TOP
10
OF
YORKSHIRE

A CORNUCOPIA OF FASCINATING FACTS ABOUT GOD'S OWN COUNTY

MIKE FOX

GREAT-N-ORTHERN

TO KATE, MEG AND MILLIE

Great Northern Books
PO Box 213, Ilkley, LS29 9WS
www.greatnorthernbooks.co.uk

ISBN: 978-0-9572951-3-1

Design and layout: David Burrill

Printed in Great Britain by CPI Group (UK)
Ltd, Croydon, CR0 4YY

CIP Data
A catalogue for this book is available from
the British Library

CONTENTS

SCHOOLS and COLLEGES   103

HISTORY   109

TOURISM, PLACES OF INTEREST, LANDSCAPE AND LEISURE

INTRODUCTION

I've always been proud to be a Yorkshire man, even when I lived in London and people used to make fun of my accent. Writing this book has made me prouder still. Yorkshire really is full of great places and great people. It has a magnificent history. The county is widely regarded as the most beautiful in the country. Its people are the friendliest and happiest, three of them have become prime ministers. Nine Oscars have been won by Yorkshire folk. Add to that seven, yes seven, Nobel Prizes and eleven Olympic gold medals. Yorkshire produces the country's favourite beers. Many of the world's greatest inventions and discoveries were made by Tykes. And let's not forget that Yorkshire was the birthplace of club football and rugby league.

I thought I knew my home county quite well, but in researching this book I realised this wasn't really the case. I've learnt a huge amount and I hope you will too. Many of the lists are subjective and you may not agree with them totally. However, I've carried out my research carefully and have given much consideration to the content and ordering of the entries. Some lists are more subjective than others and to some degree reflect my own opinions - for example the list of prettiest villages. A Facebook page has been set up so you can add your comments and opinions and I'm looking forward to hearing them. Like most Yorkshire folk I'm fond of a good debate and I'm sure that sections of this book will spark one.

Read on to find out exactly why Yorkshire is the greatest county in England.

Mike Fox

www.facebook.com/toptenofyorkshire

PEOPLE

Greatest Yorkshire men of all time

This is a very difficult list to compile. Nevertheless, this is my top ten and I've based it on two criteria; historical significance and achievements.

1. **Captain James Cook**
   1728-79. Born in Marton near Middlesbrough. He was the son of a farm labourer and rose through the ranks of the Royal Navy to become Great Britain's greatest explorer, perhaps even the world's greatest explorer. He went on three voyages of discovery to the Pacific and mapped in detail the east coast of Australia, New Zealand and the Hawaiian islands. He was killed in Hawaii by locals. They stripped his body of flesh and disembowelled him. His remains were returned to his crew and were buried at sea.

2. **William Wilberforce**
   1759-1833. Born in Hull. Member of Parliament who campaigned for the abolition of the slave trade and slavery in the British empire. The slave trade was abolished in 1807, but it was not until 1833 that an act was passed giving freedom to all slaves in the British empire. Wilberforce is buried in Westminster Abbey.

3. **John Harrison**
   1693-1776. Born in Foulby near Wakefield. Invented the marine chronometer which allowed ships to calculate longitude thereby making long distance sea travel much safer.

4. **Sir John Cockcroft**
   1897-1967. Born in Todmorden. Shared the Nobel Prize in Physics with Ernest Walton for splitting the atomic nucleus in 1932. He was instrumental in the development of nuclear power.

5. **Harry Brearley**
   1871-1948. Invented stainless steel in 1913. He was born
   into a poor family who lived in one room at the back of
   Spital Street in Sheffield. He left school at 12 and worked
   as a cellar lad and then as a bottle washer. He began to
   study metallurgy and eventually was able to set up a
   research lab. In 1913 he discovered that adding chromium
   to molten iron produced a metal that did not rust.

6. **Sir George Cayley**
   1773-1857. Born in Scarborough. He is sometimes called
   the Father of Aviation and is one of the most important
   people in the history of aeronautics. He was the first man
   to understand the underlying principles and forces of flight.
   In 1853 he designed and built the first working, piloted
   glider. The first flight was across Brompton Dale, eight
   miles west of Scarborough.

7. **John Smeaton**
   1724-92. Born in Austhorpe, Leeds. He was one of the
   first people to call himself a civil engineer. He laid the
   foundations for the profession of civil engineering. He built
   the third Eddystone lighthouse and a great many bridges,
   canals and harbours.

8. **Joseph Priestley**
   1733-1804. Born Birstall near Batley. Minister, teacher,
   scientist. Discovered oxygen and invented carbonated
   water.

9. **Sir Titus Salt**
   1803-76. Born in Morley near Leeds. Mill owner who by
   the 1840s was the largest employer in Bradford. Unhappy
   with the dreadful conditions his workers lived in, Titus built
   the model village of Saltaire and Salts Mill three miles out
   of the city centre.

10. **Joseph Rowntree**

1836-1926. Born in York. Chocolatier, but perhaps best known for being a champion of social reform. He wanted to improve the quality of life of his employees and this led him to become a philanthropist, supporting many charitable causes.

Greatest Yorkshire women of all time

1. **Sue Ryder**

1924-2000. Born in Leeds. She served with the Special Operations Executive (SOE) during the Second World War. Established by Winston Churchill in 1940, the SOE promoted and co-ordinated resistance in German occupied Europe. After the war Ryder volunteered to do relief work in Poland, France and Germany. In 1953 she established the Sue Ryder Foundation, which became Sue Ryder Care and in 2011 Sue Ryder. The charity operates homes for the sick and disabled.

Sue Ryder was appointed OBE in 1957. She was made a life peer in 1979, being created Baroness Ryder of Warsaw.

2. **Amy Johnson**

1903-1941. Born in Hull. Pioneering aviator. She was the first female pilot to fly alone from Britain to Australia in 1930. The Gypsy Moth aircraft she used can be seen in the National Science Museum. In the 1930s she set numerous long distance records. All of her accomplishments were well recognised at the time and she became a big celebrity of the day. Johnson flew in the

Second World War as part of the Air Transport Auxiliary. In 1941 whilst flying for the ATA she crashed into the Thames estuary and drowned. Her body was never recovered.

3. **Beryl Burton**
1937-96. Born in the Halton area of Leeds. Perhaps the greatest British cyclist ever. On the domestic scene Beryl ruled the roost for a quarter of a century between 1959 and 1983. She won no fewer than 96 national titles in pursuit and time trialling. Beryl also won seven world road race and pursuit titles. Had the world championships then included a time trial, as it does now, she might have won many more titles. Olympics? Well, women's cycling wasn't introduced until Beryl was 47 years old.

4. **Emily Bronte**
1818-48. Born in Thornton near Bradford. Best remembered for *Wuthering Heights*, which was her only novel. The book is a classic of English literature. It's about the passionate but doomed love between Catherine Earnshaw and Heathcliffe. Emily died of tuberculosis and was laid to rest in the family vault in Haworth church.

5. **Charlotte Bronte**
1816-55. Born in Thornton. Author of *Jane Eyre*. She also wrote the novels *Shirley* and *Villette*. In 1854 Charlotte married and fell pregnant. Sadly, she died, along with her unborn child. The death certificate gives the cause of death as tuberculosis, however there are reasons to think that she died from typhus or even dehydration and malnourishment brought on by severe morning sickness. Charlotte is interred in the family vault in Haworth church.

6. **Anne Bronte**
1820-49. Born in Thornton. Anne is overshadowed by her older sisters but her two novels, *Agnes Grey* and *The Tenant of Wildfell Hall* are still considered classics of

English literature. Haworth was not a healthy place to live. After burying Emily, Anne fell ill and travelled to Scarborough in the hope that the sea air would bring about a recovery. It did not and Anne's surviving sister, Charlotte, decided to "lay the flower where it had fallen". Anne was buried at St. Mary's churchyard in Scarborough.

7. **Anita Lonsbrough**
Born 1941 in York. Gold medal winner in the 200m breaststroke at the 1960 Rome Olympic Games. She won the race in world record time. Lonsbrough was the last British woman to win Olympic gold in swimming until Rebecca Adlington in 2008.

In 1962 she won European gold and three British Empire and Commonwealth Games golds. Later in that year Lonsbrough became the first female winner of BBC Sports Personality of the Year. Not bad for an office clerk employed at Huddersfield Town Hall.

8. **St. Hilda of Whitby**
614-680. Her actual name was Hild of Streonshal (Streonshal was the old name for Whitby). In 627 she was baptized a Christian in York. In 647 she became a nun and in 657 she founded a monastery at Whitby. The abbey became a centre of both religion and of learning. Hild presided over the Synod of Whitby in 644 which settled the differences between the Roman church and the Celtic church. Detail of Hild's life come from The Ecclesiastical History of the English by the Venerable Bede.

9. **Barbara Hepworth**
1903-75. Born in Wakefield. She was a sculptor who helped develop modern art in Britain. In 1939 Hepworth moved to St. Ives in Cornwall where she became a leading light in the town's famous artistic community after World War Two. After her death in 1975 her gallery was

transformed into the Barbara Hepworth Museum. In 1980 this became part of the Tate St. Ives. A new £35 million museum dedicated to Hepworth, The Hepworth Wakefield, opened in May 2011.

10. **Barbara Taylor Bradford**
Born 1933 in Leeds. Her debut novel, *A Woman of Substance*, was published in 1979 and has sold over 30 million copies worldwide. To date she has written 27 novels and all have been bestsellers on both sides of the Atlantic.

INDUSTRIALISTS, ENTREPRENEURS AND RETAILERS

1. **Sir Titus Salt**
Born in Morley near Leeds in 1803. Died 1876.
Titus took over his father's business in 1833 and within 20 years his textile company was the biggest employer in Bradford. Between 1801 and 1851 the population of Bradford had risen from 13,000 to 104,000. Much of the population lived in horrendous conditions and Titus, who owned five mills in Bradford, was concerned about this. He therefore relocated to an area outside of Bradford near Shipley. He built the world's biggest mill and a model community called Saltaire on the banks of the river Aire. His workers had good houses, their own outside toilets, clean drinking water and gas for lighting and heating. Saltaire had its own park, church, school, library and hospital. Titus Salt made sure that his workers were happy and healthy.

2. Joseph Rowntree

Son of a Quaker grocer, born in York in 1834. Died 1925. He started working in his father's business and in 1869 he joined his brother, Henry, who owned a chocolate factory in York. Henry died in 1883 and Joseph became the owner of the company. By the end of the 19th Century Rowntree's employed over 4,000 people.

Joseph Rowntree was a social reformer who was concerned about the conditions that many people in York lived in. He did much to improve the lives of his employees. He provided free education and free medical and dental care for his workers. In 1901 he purchased 123 acres of land at New Earswick to build houses for low income families. In 1906 he donated £10,000 to establish a pension fund for his workers.

3. Samuel Cunliffe Lister

Born at Calverley Old Hall near Bradford in 1815. Died at Swinton Park in 1906.

Lister played a key role in the development of Bradford's wool industry in the 19th Century. In 1838 he and his brother John started as worsted spinners and manufacturers in a new mill that their father built for them. This was Lister's Mill in the Manningham area of Bradford.

Samuel Lister was a very clever man and he invented the Lister nip comb which revolutionised the worsted industry and turned Bradford into the worsted capital of the world. In 1891 he was made a peer and took his title from the town of Masham which is near Swinton Park, a property he purchased in 1888. A statue of him stands in Lister Park, Bradford.

4. George Hudson -The Railway King

Born 1800 in Howsham, North Yorkshire. Died 1871.

Hudson is the person who York has to thank for its prominent role in the railways. He used an inheritance of

£30,000 to join the York establishment and to invest in railways. In the 1830s he became friends with George Stephenson and convinced him to route the line from Newcastle to London through York, rather than bypassing it on the way to Leeds. Hudson became chairman of the York and North Midland Railway Company. England was soon in the grip of railway mania and Hudson was at the centre of things. By the mid 1840s he controlled more than 1,000 miles of railway and was dubbed "The Railway King".

Hudson's fall from grace was dramatic. It came to light that he had bribed MPs and had also misled investors over the financial state of his companies. In 1847 the value of railway shares fell dramatically and many people who had been swindled by Hudson were faced with bankruptcy. Hudson was forced to repay the money that these people had lost. When he died in 1871 the former millionaire left effects worth only £200.

5. **Thomas Spencer**
Born in Skipton in 1852. Died 1905. In 1894 he joined Russian born Michael Marks to form Marks and Spencer.

In 1884 Michael Marks had opened a stall in Kirkgate Market in Leeds. Over the next few years Marks opened more market stalls across northern England. In 1894 Spencer invested £300 in Marks' activities and they opened their first store in Manchester.

6. **J. Arthur Rank**
Born in Kingston-upon-Hull in 1888. Died 1972.

Joseph Arthur Rank was an industrialist and film producer and founder of the Rank Organisation, which is now the Rank Group PLC.

His father, Joseph, set up a flour milling company in 1875. In 1899 this company became Joseph Rank Ltd. J. Arthur Rank eventually took over the family business in 1952. In 1962 the company acquired Hovis-McDougall and became Rank Hovis-McDougall Ltd.

J. Arthur Rank produced his first film, *Turn of the Tide*, in 1935. Rank also bought Heatherden Hall in Buckinghamshire and turned it into Pinewood Studios. In 1937 Rank consolidated his movie making businesses in one company called the Rank Organisation. In 1938 it took over the Odeon cinema chain and in 1942 the Paramount cinema chain. Ealing Studios were acquired in 1944.

During the 1940s Rank produced some of the finest British films ever made, including *The Red Shoes*, *Henry V* and *The Rake's Progress*. From the 1950s Rank produced the Norman Wisdom films, the Doctor films and the Carry On films.

7. **Sir Joseph Terry**

Born 1828 in York. Died 1898.

In 1854 Joseph took over his father's confectionary company and developed it so that by the end of the 19th Century it employed over 300 people. The company was incorporated in 1895 as Joseph Terry and Sons Ltd. Joseph Terry was Lord Mayor of York on four occasions and he was knighted in 1887.

8. **Sir Ken Morrison**

Born in Bradford in 1931. He took the small grocery business established by his parents in 1899 to become the 4th largest supermarket chain in the UK. Knighted in 2000.

9. **Joshua Tetley**

Born in Armley, then a small village on the outskirts of Leeds, in 1778. Died 1859.

He founded Tetley's Brewery in Leeds in 1822. It expanded to eventually become the world's largest producer of cask ale. Tetley's merged with Carlsberg of Denmark in 1992. Tetley's brewery in Leeds closed in

2011. Falling sales were blamed. Tetley's Smoothflow is now brewed in MolsonCoor's Tadcaster plant.

Joshua Tetley is buried next to his wife in Hampsthwaite village near Harrogate.

10. **Sir David Brown**
Born in Huddersfield in 1904. Died 1993. His grandfather, David Brown, commenced business in 1860 as a general pattern maker. In 1898 David Brown began to manufacture machine cut gears. By 1921 the company was the largest worm gear manufacturer in the world. Sir David took over the running of the family business in 1931. David Brown Ltd began making tractors in 1936 in a joint venture with Harry Ferguson. The collaboration only lasted four years. David Brown had designed his own tractor and during the Second World War he produced the David Brown VAK1, which eventually sold 7,700 making him a very rich man. In 1947 Brown bought Aston Martin. The legendary DB series of cars were named after Brown, using his initials. Aston Martin won Le Mans in 1959. In 1972 Brown sold both his tractor business and Aston Martin.

POLITICIANS

This list includes three prime ministers and the man who did more to abolish slavery than anyone else.

1. **William Wilberforce**
Born 1759 in Kingston-upon-Hull. Died 1833.
Campaigned for the abolition of the slave trade. Member of Parliament for Kingston-upon-Hull (1780-84), Yorkshire (1784-1812) and Bramber (1812-1825).

2. **Harold Wilson**
Born in Huddersfield in 1916. Died 1995.
   Labour prime minister 1964-70 and again 1974-76.
Member of Parliament for Ormskirk (1945-50) and then
Huyton (1953-83).

3. **Herbert Henry Asquith**
Born in Morley in 1852. Died 1928. Liberal prime minister
1908-16. Member of Parliament for East Fife (1886-1918)
and then for Paisley (1920-24).

4. **Charles Watson-Wentworth, 2nd Marquis of
Rockingham**
Born 1782 in Wentworth near Rotherham. Died 1782. He
was a British Whig statesman, most notable for his two
terms as Prime Minister of Great Britain (1765-66 and
1782).

5. **Lady Betty Boothroyd**
Born in Dewsbury in 1929. Labour Member of Parliament
for West Bromwich (1973-74) and West Bromwich West
(1974 to 2000). Speaker of the House of Commons 1992-
2000.

6. **David Blunkett**
Born in Sheffield in 1947. Labour Member of Parliament
for Sheffield Brightside and Hillsborough (1987-2010).
Secretary of State for Education and Employment (1997-
2001), Home Secretary (2001-04) and Sec. of State for
Work and Pensions (2005).

7. **Roy Hattersley**
Born in Sheffield in 1932. Labour MP for Birmingham
Sparkbrook (1964-97). Sec. of State for Prices and
Consumer Protection (1976-79), Deputy Leader of the
Labour Party (1983-92).

8. **Vince Cable**
   Born in York in 1943. MP for Twickenham since 1997. Sec. of State for Business, Innovation and Skills since 2010.

9. **William Hague**
   Born in Rotherham 1961. Conservative MP for Richmond since 1989. Sec. of State for Wales (1997), Leader of the Conservative Party (1997-2001), Sec. of State for Foreign and Commonwealth Affairs since 2010.

10. **Frank Dobson**
   Born 1940 Dunnington, near York. MP for Holborn and St Pancras South (1979-83) and Holborn and St Pancras since 1983. Sec. of State for Health 1997-99.

ARTISTS

1. **David Hockney**
   Born 1937 in Bradford. Perhaps the world's greatest living artist. Declined a knighthood in 1990 but accepted an Order of Merit in 2012. Many of Hockney's works are housed in Salt's Mill in Saltaire.

2. **Henry Moore**
   1898-1986. Born in Castleford, the son of a coalminer. He is best known for his semi-abstract monumental bronze sculptures. His forms are usually abstractions of the human figure. His works can be seen all over the world but closer to home you can see his genius at the Yorkshire Sculpture Park and the Henry Moore Institute in Leeds.

3. **Barbara Hepworth**
   1903-75. Born in Wakefield. Along with Henry Moore, Hepworth did much to develop modern art in Britain. Perhaps her best known piece is Single Form which stands outside the United Nations building in New York. The Hepworth Wakefield contains over 40 models in plaster and aluminium from the Hepworth Estate. You can also visit the Barbara Hepworth Museum and Sculpture Garden in St. Ives which is owned and run by Tate. It contains the largest collection of her work permanently on display in the house and garden where she lived and worked from 1949 to 1975.

4. **Sir Francis Leggatt Chantrey**
   1781-1841. Born in Norton near Sheffield. Sculptor. Chantrey's works are numerous and very well known. His best known works include the statues of George Washington in the State House at Boston, George III in The Guildhall, London, James Watt in Westminster Abbey and George IV in Trafalgar Square.

5. **John Flaxman**
   1755-1826. Born in York. Artist, sculptor and designer. He was the leading artist of the neoclassical style in England. When he was 19 he was employed by Josiah Wedgwood to design patterns for his china tableware. Flaxman was probably the most significant artist employed by Josiah Wedgwood. Later in his life he became famous for his memorial sculptures, which included one for Lord Nelson at St. Paul's Cathedral. He became a member of the Royal Academy in 1800 and its first professor of sculpture in 1810.

   The University College of London has The Flaxman Gallery. The gallery was host to scenes in the film *Inception* which starred Leonardo di Caprio.

6. **William Etty**

   1787-1849. Born in York. Best known for his paintings of nudes. He was financially successful in his lifetime and won royal portrait commissions despite being criticised in the press for indecency, not in his private life, but of the vast canvases of explicit nudes he painted. There is a life-sized sculpture of Etty outside York Art Gallery which contains many of his works. In 1842 Etty established the York School of Design which later became the York School of Art.

7. **Patrick Heron**

   1920-99. Born in Headingley, Leeds. Based himself at St. Ives in Cornwall.

   The *Guardian* newspaper called Heron a genius and one of the six most important British artists of the 20th Century. His works are exhibited all over the country, including the Tate Gallery London, the National Portrait Gallery, the Victoria and Albert Museum and the Leeds City Art Gallery.

8. **John Hoyland**

   1934-2011. Born in Sheffield. Hoyland was one of the country's leading abstract artists. He was elected to the Royal Academy in 1991 and was appointed Professor of the Royal Academy Schools in 1999. You can see a portrait of him in the National Portrait Gallery. The Tate holds some of his works.

9. **Sir William Rothenstein**

   1872-1945. Born in Bradford. Rothenstein is best known for his portrait drawings of famous individuals and for being an official war artist in both World War I and World War II

10. **Thomas Creswick**

    1811-1869. Born in Sheffield. Landscape painter.

INVENTORS

The mousetrap, cat's eyes, stainless steel, fizzy water and the modern computer - all from Yorkshire.

1. **John Harrison**
   1693-1776. Born in Foulby, near Wakefield. He invented the marine chronometer. This allowed ships to accurately plot their position of longitude at sea. The problem of working out longitude at sea was thought to be so intractable that the British government offered a prize of £20,000 (about £3 million today) for the solution.

2. **Harry Brearley**
   1871-1948. Born in Sheffield. Invented stainless steel. In the years before World War One arms manufacturing increased greatly and a solution to the problem of corroding gun barrels was sought. It was Brearley who added chromium to steel to produce "rustless steel" in 1913. A cutlery maker later suggested the term stainless steel.

3. **Joseph Bramah**
   1748-1814. Born in Wentworth. Inventor of the hydraulic press. Bramah was famous for many inventions including an unpickable lock, a type of flush toilet, a machine for automatically printing banknotes with sequential serial numbers and a beer pump. Bramah was a leading inventor of the industrial revolution. Many of his inventions are on display at the National Science Museum. The Bramah lock was decades ahead of any Chubb or Yale lock.

   He founded Bramah and Co. in London in 1784. The company still exists today as Bramah Security Equipment Ltd.

4. **Percy Shaw**
   1890-1976. Born in Halifax. Invented cat's eyes (reflective road studs) in 1934. In 1933 Shaw was driving home through fog from the Old Dolphin pub in Queensbury, Bradford. He was on the verge of veering off the road when his headlights caught the eyes of a cat sitting on the verge. Inspiration struck Percy. Realising how reflective the cat's eyes were he set to work to mimic them. The following year he patented a design of two reflective studs set in an iron shoe encased in rubber. His invention has probably saved hundreds of thousands of lives.

5. **Tom Kilburn**
   Born in Dewsbury in 1921. Died 2001. In the 1940s the development of electronic computers was being held up because there was no method of storing programs. Kilburn, along with Professor Sir Freddie Williams, solved this problem by creating the world's first stored-program computer. The computer made its first successful run of a program, to find the highest factor of a number, in 1948. The program was the first example of computer software. Their computer was the direct ancestor of modern computers.

   Kilburn founded Manchester University's Department of Computer Science in 1964, becoming its first professor.

6. **Joseph Aspdin**
   Born in the Hunslet district of Leeds in 1788. Died 1855. He was a bricklayer who in 1824 invented Portland cement, so called because of its similarity to Portland stone. Portland cement is the most common type of cement used around the world.

7. **James Henry Atkinson**
   1849-1942. Born in Leeds. Invented the mousetrap. It came to be known as the "Little Nipper". It's the

mousetrap that we are all familiar with. Atkinson made the traps himself but later sold the rights to Welsh company Procter Brothers for a thousand pounds. They have continued making the traps to this day.

8. **Joseph Priestley**
1733-1804. Born in Birstall near Batley. We all know that Priestley discovered oxygen but did you know that he invented soda, or carbonated water in 1770?
Unfortunately he didn't exploit the commercial potential of his invention. Others, such as J. J. Schweppe, made fortunes from it.

9. **Sir Robert Hadfield**
1858-1940. Born in Sheffield. Hadfield was a metallurgist noted for his discovery of manganese steel in 1882 and silicon steel four years later. Manganese steel was a very strong steel and was first used to make tram wheels. During World War One it was used to make armour plating, shells, tank treads and soldiers' helmets. Silicon steel was used to make electrical transformers. By 1919 15,000 people worked at Hadfields, making the company Sheffield's biggest employers.

He is commemorated in the Sir Robert Hadfield Building at the University of Sheffield which contains the Department of Materials Science and Engineering.

10. **Joseph Hansom**
Born in York in 1803. Died 1882. Invented the Hansom Cab in 1834. It was much safer than existing cabs and became the ubiquitous feature of the 19th Century street scene throughout the world.

Engineers and Mathematicians

The first glider, the Forth Bridge, the Eddystone lighthouse and the world's first underground railway were all made or engineered by Yorkshire men.

1. **Sir George Cayley**
   1773-1857. Born in Scarborough. He is sometimes called the 'Father of Aviation' and is one of the most important people in the history of aeronautics. He was the first man to understand the underlying principles and forces of flight. In 1853 he designed and built the first working, piloted glider. The first flight was across Brompton Dale, eight miles west of Scarborough.

2. **John Smeaton**
   1724-92. Born in Leeds. He was a civil engineer who designed bridges, canals, harbours and lighthouses. He was the first self-proclaimed civil engineer and is often regarded as the father of civil engineering. His commissions included the third Eddystone Lighthouse, the Calder and Hebble Navigation, Ripon Canal, Charlestown harbour in Cornwall and Coldstream bridge over the river Tweed.
   Buried at the parish church in Whitkirk, Leeds.

3. **Joseph Locke**
   1805-60. Born in Attercliffe, Sheffield. Locke ranked alongside Robert Stephenson and Isambard Kingdom Brunel as one of the major pioneers of railway development. He built the Lancaster and Carlisle Railway, the Manchester and Sheffield Railway and the Caledonian Railway from Carlisle to Glasgow and Edinburgh.

4. **Sir John Fowler**

   1817-98. Born in Sheffield. In the 1850s and 1860s he was the engineer for the world's first underground railway - London's Metropolitan railway. In the 1880s he was the chief engineer for the Forth Railway Bridge.

5. **Sir Donald Bailey**

   1901-85. Born in Rotherham. Civil engineer who invented the Bailey bridge which is a type of portable, pre-fabricated, truss bridge. A Bailey bridge has the advantages of requiring no special tools or heavy equipment to construct. It was used extensively by British and allied forces during World War 2 and Field Marshall Montgomery is recorded as saying "That without the Bailey bridge we should not have won the war."

6. **John Ramsbottom**

   1814-97. Born in Todmorden. Created many inventions for railways including the piston ring, the Ramsbottom safety valve, the displacement lubricator and the water trough.

7. **Christopher Saxton**

   1540-1610. Born in Dewsbury. Known as "the father of English cartography". As a young man Saxton worked for John Rudd who was the vicar of Dewsbury and rector of Thornhill. Rudd was a keen cartographer and he passed on his skills to Saxton. In 1574 Saxton began a survey of the whole of England and Wales on the commission of Lord Burghley who saw the national importance of effective maps. This was a massive undertaking, but by 1578 the survey was complete. The maps set the standard for all other cartographers to follow. As the first man to fully survey England and Wales, Saxton's contribution to cartography are second to none.

8. **John Metcalfe - "Blind Jack of Knaresborough".**
   1717-1810. Born in Knaresborough. Metcalfe was a blind
   engineer who designed and built some of Britain's earliest
   modern roads. He lost his sight after contracting smallpox
   at the age of 6. This didn't stop him running a coaching
   business between York and Knaresborough. Following the
   Turnpike Act of 1752 Blind Jack won a contract to build
   three miles of road from Ferrensby to Minskip near
   Knaresborough. This was the start of a road building
   career which saw him build 180 miles of roads across
   northern England. A statue of him was erected in
   Knaresborough's market place in 2009 after residents had
   raised £30,000.

9. **Henry Briggs**
   1561-1630. Born in Warley Wood near Halifax. Do you
   remember logarithms from your geometry lessons? Those
   boring afternoons are all down to Briggs who invented and
   popularised logarithms to base ten, which are now called
   common logarithms or Briggsian logarithms. Logarithms
   were actually invented by John Napier, but Briggs made
   them easier to use by converting them to base ten. I won't
   try to explain this here.

10. **John Venn**
    1834-1923. Born in Hull. Famous for inventing the Venn
    diagram. Venn was also skilled at building machines. One
    machine he built could bowl cricket balls. It was so good
    that when the Australian cricket team visited England in
    1909 it clean bowled one of its top batters four times.

Scientists

Big bang theory, the discovery of oxygen, genetics, anaesthetics and the splitting of the atomic nucleus. Yorkshire people have been responsible for some of the greatest developments in science and medicine. The county has produced at least seven Nobel Prize winners. Two have come from the same school - Todmorden High.

1. **Sir John Cockroft**
   Born in Todmorden in 1897. Died 1967. He was one of the greatest physicists of all time and he shared the Nobel Prize in Physics with Ernest Walton for splitting the atomic nucleus, which they achieved in 1932 at Cambridge University. He was also instrumental in the development of nuclear power.

2. **Joseph Priestley**
   Born in Birstall near Batley in 1733. Died 1804. Priestley was a church minister and claimed that his scientific research was just a hobby. He discovered oxygen and invented carbonated water, though he did not exploit its commercial potential.

3. **Sir Fred Hoyle**
   Born in Gilstead near Bingley in 1915. Died 2001. Astronomer and mathematician noted primarily for his contribution to the theory of stellar nucleosynthesis - this explains how heavier than hydrogen atoms are formed inside stars. All the atoms that exist, including the ones that make up this book, the air you breathe and you, are made inside stars.

   He also coined the term "Big Bang" in 1949, even though he rejected the theory.

4. **John Snow**

Born in York in 1813. Died 1858. He was a doctor who pioneered the use of ether and chloroform as anaesthetics, which allowed patients to undergo operations without the distress and pain they would otherwise suffer. Snow is also considered to be one of the fathers of modern epidemiology because of his work in tracing the source of the cholera outbreak in Soho in 1854. In a poll of British doctors in 2003 he was voted the greatest physician of all time .

5. **Sir Edward Victor Appleton**

Born in Bradford in 1892. Died 1965. He discovered the ionosphere and his findings allowed others to develop radar, a crucial weapon against the German Luftwaffe during World War 2. In 1947 Appleton was awarded the Nobel Prize in Physics.

6. **Adam Sedgwick**

1785-1873. Born in Dent which is now part of Cumbria, although when Sedgwick was born the village was in the West Riding of Yorkshire. He was one of the founders of modern geology. He was a prominent researcher and teacher in what has been called the Heroic Age of Geology. This was the time when the great geological periods were defined and when much exploration and fundamental research was carried out. The Sedgwick Museum of Earth Sciences is the geology museum of Cambridge University. There's also a memorial to Sedgwick in Dent.

7. **Sir Geoffrey Wilkinson**

Born in Todmorden in 1921. Died 1996. Wilkinson pioneered inorganic chemistry. He won the Nobel Prize in Chemistry in 1973 for his work on organometallic compounds.

Amazingly, both Wilkinson and John Cockroft went to Todmorden Secondary School and were taught physics by Luke Sutcliffe.

8. **Sir Nevill Mott**
1905-96. Born in Leeds. Mott's accomplishments include explaining the effect of light on photographic emulsions. Mott transition, Mott insulators and Mott polynomials are all named after him. He was awarded the Nobel Prize in Physics in 1977.

9. **George Birkbeck**
1776-1841. Born in Settle. He was a doctor, academic and pioneer in adult education. He founded Birkbeck College in London. George Birkbeck established a Mechanics' Institute in Glasgow and then in London. Mechanics' Institutes were educational establishments that provided free adult education to working men in technical subjects. The one established in London became known as Birkbeck College in 1907.

10. **William Bateson**
Born in Robin Hood's Bay in 1861. Died 1926. He studied hereditary and variation and was the first person to use the term genetics. He was also the chief populariser of the ideas of Gregor Mendel following their rediscovery in 1900.

FEMALE NOVELISTS AND POETS

The Bronte sisters are the greatest literary family the world has known. Where they lived inspired their works, but sadly, also killed them. Haworth was a very unhealthy place to live. In the early 19th Century the average life expectancy in the town was only 28 and it was racked with typhus, cholera and tuberculosis.

1. **Emily Bronte**
   Born in Thornton, Bradford in 1818. Died of tuberculosis in 1848 and is interred in the family vault at the Church of St. Michael and All Angels, Haworth. Best remembered for her only novel, *Wuthering Heights*.

2. **Charlotte Bronte**
   Born in Thornton in 1816. Died of tuberculosis in 1855. Her best known novels are *Jayne Eyre* and *Villette*.

3. **Anne Bronte**
   Born in Thornton in 1820. Died in 1849. Buried at St. Mary's Church in Scarborough. Wrote the novels *Agnes Grey* and *The Tenant of Wildfell Hall*.

4. **Barbara Taylor Bradford**
   Born in Leeds in 1933. So far, she has written 27 novels, which have all been best sellers on both sides of the Atlantic. Her debut novel, *A Woman of Substance*, was published in 1979 and has sold over 32 million copies worldwide. At school she was in the same class as Alan Bennett.

5. **Dame Edith Sitwell**
   1887-1964. Born in Scarborough. Poet and biographer. She began writing poetry in 1912 and became very well known. Her best poetry was written during World War 2

and was inspired by the Blitz. She also wrote biographies of Queen Victoria and Queen Elizabeth I. Sitwell was a strange looking woman, six feet tall with a huge beaked nose. She dressed in turbans, feathers and very odd jewellery. Renishaw Hall near Sheffield was her ancestral home. She was created Dame of the British Empire in 1954. In 1962 she was caught by Eamonn Andrews for *This is Your Life*.

6. **Helen Fielding**
   Born in Morley in 1958. Author of *Bridget Jones's Diary* and *Bridget Jones: The Edge of Reason*.

7. **Joanne Harris**
   Born in Barnsley in 1964. In 1999 she wrote *Chocolat* which reached number one in the *Sunday Times* newspaper's bestsellers list. It was made into a film starring Juliette Binoche and Johnny Depp.

8. **A. S. Byatt (Dame Antonia Susan Duffy)**
   Born in Sheffield in 1936. Won the 1990 Booker Prize for *Possession: A Romance*.

9. **Phyllis Bentley**
   Born in Halifax in 1894. Died 1977. *Inheritance* written in 1932 is her best known novel. In 1967 it became an ITV drama starring John Thaw and James Bolam.

10. **Kate Atkinson**
    Born in York in 1951. Her first novel, *Behind the Scenes at the Museum*, won the 1995 Whitbread Book of the Year. It became a *Sunday Times* bestseller. Since then she's written another five novels and in 2011 was awarded an MBE.

Male Poets

1. **W. H. Auden (Wystan Hugh Auden)**
   Born in York in 1907. Died 1973. Wrote *Funeral Blues (Stop all the Clocks)* - the poem recited at the funeral in the film *Four Weddings and a Funeral*.

2. **Ted Hughes**
   Born in Mytholmroyd in 1930. Died 1998. Hughes was British Poet Laureate from 1984 until his death. In 2008 *The Times* ranked Hughes fourth on their list of "The 50 greatest British writers since 1945".

3. **Andrew Marvell**
   Born in Winestead-in-Holderness near Kingston-Upon-Hull in 1621. Died 1678. His most famous poems include *To His Coy Mistress, The Garden* and *An Horatian Ode*. A secondary school in Hull is named after him. A statue of him is located in the city's Trinity Square. He was MP for Hull from 1659 until his death.

4. **Alfred Austin**
   Born in Headingley, Leeds in 1835. Died 1913. He was appointed Poet Laureate in 1896 upon the death of Alfred, Lord Tennyson.

5. **Sir William Empson**
   Born in Hawdon in 1906. Died 1984. Literary critic and poet. His best known work is *Seven Types of Ambiguity* published in 1930.

6. **Neil Rollinson**
   Born 1960 in Keighley. Winner of the Cholmondeley Award in 2005.

7. **Tony Harrison**

   Born 1937 in Leeds. Winner of the Cholmondeley Award in 1969.

8. **Ken Smith**

   1938-2003. Born in Rudston. Winner of the Cholmondeley Award in 1998.

9. **Blake Morrison**

   Born in Skipton 1950. Poet and author best know for his autobiography titled *And When Did You Last See Your Father?* which in 2007 was made into a film starring Colin Firth, Jim Broadbent and Juliet Stevenson.

10. **Ian McMillan**

    Born 1956 in Darfield near Barnsley. Poet in residence to his hometown football club, Barnsley FC. In 2010 appointed poet in residence at the English National Opera. Hosts a weekly BBC Radio 3 show and regularly appears on TV.

And also:

Caedmon

He's the earliest known old English poet. He was a herdsman at the monastery of Streonshal (Whitby Abbey) during the abbacy of St. Hilda in the 7th Century. According to the 8th Century monk Bede he was "originally ignorant in the art of song" but learned to compose one night in the course of a dream.

Caedmon became a monk and devoted much of his time to the writing of religious poetry.

Caedmon's only known surviving work is *Caedmon's Hymn*, the nine-line alliterative vernacular praise poem in honour of God which he supposedly learned to sing in his initial dream.

MALE NOVELISTS

1. **Arthur Ransome**
   Born in Leeds in 1884. Died 1967. He's best known for writing the *Swallows and Amazons* series of children's books.

2. **John Braine**
   1922-86. Born in Bradford. Best known for his first novel, *Room at the Top*, published in 1957, which was turned into a very successful film of the same name. He followed this up with *Life at the Top*. Braine was one of the celebrated Angry Young Men of British literature.

3. **Barry Hines**
   Born in Hoyland Common near Barnsley in 1939. He is best known for the novel *A Kestrel for a Knave*, which became the film *Kes*.

4. **Nicholas Rhea**
   Born 1936 in Glaisdale
   Nicholas Rhea is the pseudonym of Peter Walker. He wrote the *Constable* series of books that provided the inspiration for the *Heartbeat* TV series.

5. **George Gissing**
   1857-1903. Born in Wakefield. He published 23 novels and was one of the most accomplished realists of the late 19th Century. Some believe him to be one of the best three novelists of his time along with George Meredith and Thomas Hardy. However, his personal life is probably as interesting as any of his books. He fell in love with a prostitute, spent time in prison for theft and was friends with H.G. Wells. You can visit the Gissing Centre in Wakefield.

6. **G. P. Taylor**
   Born 1958 in Scarborough. Author of best-selling novels *Shadowmancer*, *Wormwood* and *Tersias*. In the 1970s he worked in the music industry with such bands as The Sex Pistols and The Stranglers. He became involved in the occult but then turned to Christianity and became a vicar.

7. **David Peace**
   Born in Ossett in 1967. Wrote the *Red Riding Quartet* which comprised the novels *Nineteen Seventy-four*, *Nineteen Seventy-Seven*, *Nineteen Eighty* and *Nineteen Eighty Three*. Peace also wrote *The Damned United*.

8. **Stan Barstow**
   1928-2011. Born in Horbury near Wakefield. Best known for his 1960 novel *A Kind of Loving* which has been used as a set text in British schools and which has been translated into a film, a TV series, a radio play and a stage play. The 1962 film was directed by John Schlesinger and starred Alan Bates and June Ritchie. In 1982 ITV made into a ten part TV series starring Clive Wood and Joanne Whalley.

9. **David Storey**
   Born in Wakefield in 1933. Wrote *This Sporting Life* in 1960. He also wrote *Saville* which won the 1976 Booker Prize.

10. **Eric Knight**
    Born in Menston in 1897. Died 1943. Wrote *Lassie Come Home* in 1940.

In addition:

Roger Hargreaves
Born in Cleckheaton in 1935. Died 1988. Wrote and illustrated the *Mr Men* and *Little Miss* series of children's books. *Mr Tickle* was the first book in 1971. He wrote 46 *Mr Men* and 33 *Little Miss* books.

PLAYWRIGHTS AND SCREENWRITERS

1. **Alan Bennett**
   Born in Armley, Leeds in 1934. He achieved fame in 1960 by writing and acting in the satirical revue *Beyond the Fringe* at the Edinburgh Festival. His co-stars were Dudley Moore, Jonathan Miller and Peter Cook. His later work includes the plays *The Madness of George III* (which became the film *The Madness of King George*) and *The History Boys*.

2. **J. B. Priestley (John Boynton Priestley)**
   Born in the Manningham area of Bradford in 1894. Died 1984. He wrote several plays, the best known being *An Inspector Calls* which is considered to be one of the classics of 20th Century English theatre. He also published 26 novels, including *The Good Companions* in 1929 which made him a national figure.

3. **John Godber**
   Born 1956 in Upton near Pontefract. Before becoming a playwright and director he wrote for the TV series *Crown Court, Brookside* and *Grange Hill*. He also devised the BBC series *Chalkface*. He has written many plays including *Up 'n' Under* (which was turned into a film), *Bouncers* and *Teechers* (not a misprint). He is reckoned to be the third most frequently performed British playwright after Shakespeare and Alan Ayckbourn.

4. **William Congreve**
   1670-1729. Born in Bardsey near Leeds. Congreve wrote some of the most popular English plays of the late 17th Century including *Love for Love* and *The Way of the World*.

5. **Roy Clarke**
Born in Austerfield, near Doncaster in 1930. Best known for creating TV sitcoms *Last of the Summer Wine*, *Open All Hours* and *Keeping Up Appearances*.

6. **Kay Mellor**
Born 1951 in Leeds. She wrote the TV series *Band of Gold* and *Playing the Field*. Mellor also created the series *Fat Friends* and wrote and directed the film *Fanny and Elvis* that starred Ray Winstone. Awarded the OBE in 2009.

7. **Keith Waterhouse**
Born in Hunslet, Leeds in 1929. Died 2009.
   In 1959 he wrote the novel *Billy Liar*. Waterhouse adapted the book into a stage play, a film and a TV series. He also wrote many other TV shows. His credits include *That Was The Week That Was*, *The Frost Report*, *Budgie* and *Worzel Gummidge*.

8. **Simon Beaufoy**
Born in Keighley in 1967. In 2009 he won the Oscar for Best Adapted Screenplay for *Slumdog Millionaire*. He also wrote the screenplays for *The Full Monty* and *127 Hours*.

9. **John Arden**
Born in Barnsley in 1930. Best known for his 1959 play *Serjeant Musgrave's Dance*

10. **Willis Hall**
1929-2005. Born in Leeds. Co-wrote the screenplay for *Billy Liar* with his friend Keith Waterhouse. Made his name and fame with the play *The Long And The Short And The Tall*. Hall wrote prolifically for radio and TV (including *Minder*) and also wrote a dozen children's books.

Famous men from Leeds (living)

(On the next few pages most of the people mentioned were born in the city or town in the title, but a few were born in nearby villages.)

1. **Alan Bennett**. Born 1934. Playwright.
2. **John Craven**. Born 1940. TV presenter.
3. **Malcolm McDowell**. Born 1943. Actor - *A Clockwork Orange*.
4. **Ray Illingworth**. Born 1932. Cricketer - Yorkshire and England captain.
5. **Chris Moyles**. Born 1974. Ex-Radio 1 DJ.
6. **Jeremy Paxman**. Born 1950. TV presenter - Newsnight and University Challenge.
7. **John Simm**. Born 1970. Actor - best known for playing Sam Tyler in *Life on Mars*.
8. **Marco Pierre White**. Born 1961. Celebrity chef.
9. **Brian Close**. Born 1931. Cricketer - Yorkshire and England captain. Youngest ever to play test cricket for England.
10. **Leigh Francis**. Born 1973. Creator of *Bo' Selecta!* and Keith Lemon.

Famous men from Leeds (deceased)

1. **Richard Oastler** 1789-1861. Oastler was an early campaigner against slavery in the West Indies but in the 1830s he turned his attention to the exploitation of textile workers in Britain. His 1830 letter to the Leeds Mercury about "Yorkshire Slavery" began the campaign to reduce the working day of factory children to ten hours. His tireless campaigning eventually led to The Ten Hours Act of 1847.
2. **Herbert Asquith**. 1852-1928. Liberal prime minister from 1908 to 1916.
3. **Arthur Ransome**. 1884-1967. Author of *Swallows and Amazons*.
4. **Ernie Wise**. 1925-1999. One half of Morecambe and Wise.
5. **Sir Len Hutton**. 1916-1990. Cricketer - one of the greatest batsmen of all time.
6. **Alfred Austin**. 1835-1913. Poet Laureate.
7. **Sir Titus Salt**. 1803-1876. Businessman and philanthropist. Built Saltaire which is now a World Heritage Site.
8. **Hedley Verity**. 1905-1943. Cricketer - in 1932 took ten wickets for ten runs in a match against Nottinghamshire. Still a world record.
9. **Gordon Pirie**. 1931-1991. Olympic silver medallist in the 5000m at the 1956 Melbourne games. BBC Sports Personality of the Year 1955. World record holder in the 5000m and 3000m.
10. **Keith Waterhouse**. 1929-2009. Novelist and writer for television.

Famous women from Leeds

1. **Sue Ryder**. 1924-2000. Special Operations Executive in the Second World War and founder of the charity that bears her name.
2. **Beryl Burton**. 1937-1996. World champion cyclist.
3. **Barbara Taylor Bradford**. Born 1933. Novelist. She was in the same class at school as Alan Bennett.
4. **Gaby Logan**. Born 1973. TV presenter. Daughter of Leeds Utd footballer Terry Yorath.
5. **Nell McAndrew**. Born 1973. Model. Also a very good amateur athlete with a best time for the marathon of two hours 54 minutes.
6. **Kay Mellor**. Born 1951. Writer of TV dramas such as *Band of Gold, Fat Friends* and *The Syndicate*.
7. **Helen Fielding**. Born 1958. Author of *Bridget Jones' Diary*.
8. **Corinne Bailey Rae**. Born 1979. Singer/songwriter.
9. **Melanie Brown**. Born 1975. Spice Girl.
10. **Gaynor Faye**. Born 1971. Actress. Daughter of Kay Mellor.

Famous men from Sheffield

1. **Gordon Banks**. Born 1937. England 1966 World Cup winning goalkeeper. Known as "The Banks of England".
2. **Michael Palin**. Born 1943. Writer, actor, travel broadcaster.
3. **Sean Bean**. Born 1959. Actor.
4. **Harry Brearley**. 1871-1948. Invented stainless steel.
5. **Naseem Hamed**. Born 1974. Boxer - former world featherweight champion.
6. **Roger Taylor**. Born 1941. Tennis player - Wimbledon semi-finalist three times.

7. **Howard Wilkinson**. Born 1943. Last English manager to win the top flight league in England (with Leeds Utd in 1992).
8. **Jarvis Cocker**. Born 1963. Lead singer with Pulp.
9. **Sir Alastair Burnet**. 1928-2012. News at Ten presenter.
10. **Joe Cocker**. Born 1944. Singer/songwriter. 1983 Grammy Award winner for his hit "Up Where We Belong", a duet he performed with Jennifer Warnes.

FAMOUS WOMEN FROM SHEFFIELD

1. **Dame Antonia Susan Duffy (A. S. Byatt)**. Born 1936. Novelist and poet.
2. **Helen Sharman**. Born 1963. First Briton in space.
3. **Jessica Ennis**. Born 1986. Athlete. 2012 Olympic heptathlon champion.
4. **Margaret Drabble**. Born 1939. Novelist. Sister of A. S. Byatt.
5. **Marti Caine**. 1944-1995. Comedienne.
6. **Sheila Sherwood**. Born 1945. Long jumper - won silver at the 1968 Mexico City Olympics.
7. **Jessica-Jane Clement**. Born 1985. Model and TV presenter - *The Real Hustle, I'm a Celebrity... Get me out of here*.
8. **Oona King**. Born 1967. Former Labour Party MP. She was the second black female MP elected to the House of Commons, after Diane Abbott.
9. **Charlotte Hudson**. Born 1972. TV presenter - *Brainiac: History Abuse* on Sky 1.
10. **Nicola Minichiello**. Born in Sheffield in 1978. World bobsleigh champion in 2009.

Famous People From Doncaster

1. **Thomas Crapper**. 1836-1910. Plumber who founded Thomas Crapper & Co in London. Contrary to widespread belief, Crapper did not invent the flush toilet. He did, however, do much to increase the popularity of the toilet by developing some important related inventions, such as the ballcock. He was noted for the quality of his products and received several royal warrants.
2. **Kevin Keegan**. Born 1951. Footballer.
3. **Roy Clarke**. Born 1930. Comedy writer - *Last of the Summer Wine, Open All Hours*.
4. **Jeremy Clarkson**. Born 1960. Journalist and TV presenter - *Top Gear*.
5. **Brian Blessed**. Born 1936. Actor.
6. **Tony Christie**. Born 1943. Singer - *Is this the way to Amarillo? Avenues and Alleyways*.
7. **James Toseland**. Born 1980. Superbike World Champion 2004 and 2007.
8. **Lesley Garrett**. Born 1955. Soprano singer.
9. **Diana Rigg**. Born 1938. Actress - Emma Peel in *The Avengers*.
10. **Sarah Stevenson**. Born 1983. Taekwondo athlete - world champion in 2001 and 2011. Olympic bronze medallist in 2008.

Famous People From Bradford

1. **Sir Edward Appleton**. 1892-1965. Physicist and Nobel prize winner.
2. **Emily Bronte**. 1818-1848. Novelist - *Wuthering Heights*.
3. **Charlotte Bronte**. 1816-1855. Novelist - *Jane Eyre*.
4. **Anne Bronte**. 1820-1849. Novelist - *The Tenant of Wildfell Hall*.
5. **David Hockney**. Born 1937. Painter.

6. **Frederick Delius**. 1862-1934. Composer.
7. **J. B. Priestley**. 1894-1984. Novelist and playwright - *An Inspector Calls*.
8. **Richard Whiteley**. 1943-2005. TV presenter - *Countdown*.
9. **Harry Corbett**. 1918-1989. Creator of *Sooty and Sweep*.
10. **Ade Edmondson**. Born 1957. Comic actor and TV presenter.

Famous people from Rotherham

1. **Sir Donald Bailey**. 1901-1985. Civil engineer who invented the Bailey bridge.
2. **Herbert Chapman**. 1878-1934. Won the old Division 1 title and the F. A. Cup as a manager with Huddersfield Town and Arsenal.
3. **Peter Elliott**. Born 1962. Won silver in the 1500m at the 1988 Seoul Olympics.
4. **Paul Goodison**. Born 1977. Won gold in laser class sailing at the 2009 Beijing Olympics. Was also 2009 world champion.
5. **William Hague**. Born in 1961. Former Conservative Party leader and current Foreign Secretary. MP for Richmond.
6. **Gervase Phinn**. Born 1946. Former teacher and schools inspector. Now an author.
7. **David Seaman**. Born 1963. Former England goalkeeper.
8. **Paul Shane**. Born 1940. Comedian and actor. Best known for his role in *Hi-De-Hi*.
9. **Ben Swift**. Born 1987. 2012 world champion in track cycling.
10. **Howard Webb**. Born 1971. Football referee. Refereed the 2010 World Cup final.

Famous people from Scarborough

1. **Sir George Cayley**. 1773-1857. Pioneer of aeronautical engineering and the first person to build and fly a glider.
2. **Charles Laughton** 1899–1962. Oscar winning actor.
3. **Bill Nicholson**. 1919-2004. Football manager who won the League and F. A. Cup double with Spurs in 1961.
4. **Sir Ben Kingsley**. Born 1943. Oscar winning actor.
5. **G.P. Taylor**. Born 1958. Author - *Shadowmancer, Wormwood.*
6. **Selina Scott**. Born 1951. Journalist and TV presenter.
7. **Paul Ingle**. Born 1972. Boxer - former IBF featherweight world champion.
8. **Sir Edward Harland**. 1831-1895. Founder of Belfast shipbuilding company Harland and Wolff which built the Titanic.
9. **Susan Hill**. Born 1942. Novelist - *The Woman in Black, I'm the King of the Castle.*
10. **Dame Edith Sitwell**. 1887-1964. Poet.

(Alan Ayckbourn was born in London)

Famous people from Halifax

1. **Richard Dunn**. Born 1945. Heavyweight boxer. Fought Muhammad Ali in 1976.
2. **Percy Shaw**. 1890-1976. Invented cat's eyes.
3. **Ted Hughes**. 1930-1998. Poet Laureate from 1984 until his death.
4. **Sir John Cockcroft**. 1897-1967. Physicist. Won the Nobel Prize in Physics for splitting the atomic nucleus with Ernest Walton.

5. **Sir Geoffrey Wilkinson**. 1921-1996. Won the Nobel Prize for Chemistry. Went to the same school in Todmorden as John Cockcroft.
6. **John Noakes**. Born 1934. *Blue Peter* presenter from 1965 to 1978 (still the show's longest serving presenter).
7. **Henry Briggs**. 1561-1630. Mathematician. Notable for changing the original logarithms invented by John Napier into common (base 10) logarithms, which are sometimes known as Briggsian logarithms in his honour.
8. **Oliver Smithies**. Born 1925. He is a geneticist who in 1955 invented gel electrophoresis. He also developed techniques for altering animal genomes and inserting human genes into mice. Smithies' work has advanced research in cystic fibrosis and could possibly have applications in other human diseases. He was awarded the Nobel Prize in Physiology or Medicine in 2007.
9. **Sir Bernard Ingham**. Born 1932. Margaret Thatcher's chief press secretary while she was prime minister.
10. **Big Daddy** (Shirley Crabtree). 1930-1997. Wrestler.

FAMOUS PEOPLE FROM KEIGHLEY

1. **Alastair Campbell**. Born 1957. Director of communications and strategy for Prime Minister Tony Blair between 1997 and 2003.
2. **Simon Beaufoy**. Born 1967. Oscar winning screenwriter - *Slumdog Millionaire*.
3. **Mollie Sugden**. 1922-2009. Comedy actress - Mrs Slocombe in *Are You Being Served?*
4. **Eric Pickles**. Born 1952. Secretary of State for Communities and Local Government.
5. **Paul Hudson**. Born 1971. BBC weather presenter.
6. **Margaret Wintringham**. 1879-1955. Liberal Party MP. She was the second woman to be elected to the House of Commons.

7. **Ricky Wilson**. Born 1978. Lead singer of the Kaiser Chiefs.
8. **Timothy Taylor**. Founded the brewery bearing his name in 1858.
9. **Gordon Bottomley**. 1874-1948. Poet.
10. **Mike Hellawell**. Born 1938. Footballer. Played twice for England in 1962.

Famous people from Wakefield

1. **John Harrison**. 1693-1776. Invented the marine chronometer.
2. **Barbara Hepworth**. 1903-1975. Sculptor.
3. **Henry Moore**. 1898-1986. Sculptor.
4. **Geoffrey Boycott**. Born 1940. Cricketer.
5. **David Storey**. Born 1933. Former professional rugby league player and author of *This Sporting Life*.
6. **Jane Tomlinson**. 1964-2007. Charity fundraiser.
7. **Stan Barstow**. 1928-2011. Author of *A Kind of Loving*.
8. **Sir Martin Frobisher**. 1535-1594. Elizabethan explorer.
9. **George Gissing**. 1857-1903. Novelist.
10. **David Mercer**. 1928-1980. Playwright for stage and TV.

Famous people from York

1. **Anita Lonsbrough**. Born 1941. swimmer – gold medallist in the 200m breaststroke at the 1960 Rome Olympics.
2. **Guy Fawkes**. 1570-1606. Planned the gunpowder plot of 1605.
3. **Dame Judy Dench**. Born 1934. Actress.
4. **W. H. Auden**. 1907-1973. Poet.
5. **Frankie Howerd**. 1917-1992. Comedian.
6. **John Barry**. 1933-2011. Composer - composed music for 12 James Bond films between 1962 and 1987.

7. **Joseph Rowntree**. 1836-1925. Quaker businessman and philanthropist.
8. **Jon Snow**. 1813-1858. Physician who pioneered the use of anaesthetics.
9. **Alcuin**. 730s or 740s to 804. Scholar, ecclesiastic, poet and teacher.
10. **Joseph Hansom**. 1803-1882. Invented the Hansom cab.

FAMOUS PEOPLE FROM HUDDERSFIELD

1. **James Mason**. 1909-1984. Actor.
2. **Harold Wilson**. 1916-1995. Twice prime minister.
3. **Roy Castle**. 1932-1994. TV presenter.
4. **Derek Ibbotson**. Born 1932. Bronze medal winner in the 5000m at the 1956 Melbourne Olympics. Also set a world record in the mile in 1957.
5. **Sir Patrick Stewart**. Born 1940. Actor.
   (from Mirfield, four miles from Huddersfield)
6. **Wilfred Rhodes**. 1877-1973. Cricketer.
7. **John Whitaker**. Born 1955. Show jumper.
8. **Sir David Brown**. 1904-1993. Tractor maker and former owner of Aston Martin.
9. **Simon Armitage**. Born 1963. Novelist, poet and playwright.
10. **Gordon Kaye**. Born 1941. Comedy actor - Rene Artois in *'Allo 'Allo!*

Famous people from Barnsley

1. **Sir Michael Parkinson**. Born 1935. Broadcaster, journalist and author.
2. **Dickie Bird**. Born 1933. Cricket umpire. At one time, Dickie Bird, Michael Parkinson and Geoffrey Boycott played together for Barnsley Cricket Club.
3. **Ed Clancy**. Born 1985. 2008 and 2012 Olympic gold medallist in track cycling team pursuit. Also a four time world champion in team pursuit.
4. **Darren Gough**. Born 1970. Cricketer.
5. **Jimmy Greenhoff**. Born 1946. Footballer. The finest player to never play for England.
6. **Arthur Scargill**. Born 1938. Former leader of the National Union of Mineworkers.
7. **Ian McMillan**. Born 1956. Poet.
8. **Barry Hines**. Born 1939. Novelist - *A Kestrel for a Knave*.
9. **Mick McCarthy**. Born 1959. Footballer.
10. **Martyn Moxon**. Born 1960. Cricketer.

Famous people from Middlesbrough

1. **James Cook**. 1728-1779. Explorer.
2. **Brian Clough**. 1935-2004. Footballer and manager.
3. **Don Revie**. 1927-1989. Footballer and manager.
4. **Chris Old**. Born 1948. Cricketer.
5. **Bob Mortimer**. 1959. Comedian and actor.
6. **Chris Rea**. Born 1951. Singer/songwriter.
7. **Wendy Richard**. 1943-2009. Actress.
8. **Rory Underwood**. Born 1963. Rugby union player.
9. **Wilf Mannion**. 1918-2000. Footballer.
10. **Paul Daniels**. Born 1938. Magician.

Famous people from Hull

1. **William Wilberforce**. 1759-1833. MP and leader of the movement to abolish the slave trade.
2. **Amy Johnson**. 1903-1941. Pioneering aviator.
3. **J. Arthur Rank**. 1888-1972. Industrialist and film producer and founder of the Rank Organisation, now known as The Rank Group Plc.
4. **Sir Tom Courtenay**. Born 1937. Actor.
5. **Maureen Lipman**. Born 1946. Actress.
6. **John Venn**. 1834-1923. Invented the Venn diagram.
7. **Ian Carmichael**. 1920-2010. Actor.
8. **Norman Collier**. Born 1925. Comic.
9. **Thomas Tomlinson**. 1838-1927. Established the Cussons brand famous for making Imperial Leather soap.
10. **Ebenezer Cobb Morley**. 1831-1924. Founding member of the F.A.

Famous people from Dewsbury

1. **Betty Boothroyd**. Born 1929. Speaker of the House of Commons 1992-2000.
2. **Andrew Morton**. Born 1953. Wrote a biography of Princess Diana.
3. **Tom Kilburn**. 1921-2001. Along with Freddie Williams produced the world's first stored-program computer.
4. **Sir Owen Willans Richardson**. 1879-1959. Won the Nobel Prize in Physics in 1928.
5. **Christopher Saxton**. 1540-1610. Cartographer.
6. **Eddie Waring**. 1910-1986. Rugby league commentator.
7. **Andrew Gale**. Born 1983. Yorkshire cricket captain.
8. **Alistair Brownlee**. Born 1988. World triathlon champion 2009 and 2011. 2012 Olympic triathlon champion.
9. **Sir Thomas Clifford Allbutt**. 1836–1925. Physician and inventor of the clinical thermometer.

10. **Eileen Fenton**. Born 1929. In 1950 Eileen was the first woman to finish in the Daily Mail First International Cross-Channel Race. During the race, Eileen had been level with the eventual winner until an arm injury forced her to drop back.

For being the first woman to complete the race Eileen received £1000, about the price of an average house, from the *Daily Mail*.

To get used to cold water she did her training in the sea off the coast of Scarborough. She later said the Channel "seemed quite warm … after the North Coast".

The people in her home town of Dewsbury were overjoyed at her Victory. She received a hero's welcome upon her return and the streets were packed with over 20,000 celebrating well wishers.

Famous Yorkshire residents, or former residents not born in Yorkshire (living)

1. Sir Alan Ayckbourn

Born 1939 in Hampstead, London. Playwright who lives in Scarborough. He has written over 70 plays and between 1972 and 2009 was the artistic director of the Stephen Joseph Theatre in Scarborough where most of his plays have had their first performance.

2. Peter O'Toole

Probably born 1932 in Connemara in Ireland. He achieved stardom in 1962 by playing T.E. Lawrence in the film *Lawrence of Arabia*. Brought up in Leeds and on leaving school he worked as a trainee journalist and photographer on the *Yorkshire Evening Post*. After national service he went to RADA where he was in the same class as Albert Finney and Alan Bates. O'Toole has been nominated eight times for the Academy Award for best actor in a leading role. He is the most nominated actor to never win the award.

3. **Dennis Healey**
Born 1917 in London. Moved with his family to Keighley when he was 5. Member of Parliament for Leeds South-East 1952-55 and for Leeds East 1955-92. Secretary of State for Defence 1964-70 and Chancellor of the Exchequer 1974-79. Healey was educated at Bradford Grammar School. After World War 2 he lived with his wife in East Sussex. Although being MP for Leeds for 40 years he never bought a house in the city, instead he chose to stay with friends whilst on constituency business. In 1992 he received a life peerage as Baron Healey of Riddlesden, which is a village near Keighley.

4. **Michael Vaughan**
Born 1974 in Salford. Moved to Sheffield when he was 8. England cricket captain in 51 tests between 2003 and 2008. Vaughan is the most successful captain in the history of English cricket and was a former world number one batsman.

5. **Damien Hirst**
Born 1965 in Bristol. Britain's richest living artist. According to the *Sunday Times* rich list he is worth £215million. Hirst grew up in Leeds. He attended Allerton Grange High School and only achieved an E grade in A-level art. Hirst then went to Leeds College of Art and Design.

6. **Bill Bryson**
Born 1951 in Iowa, USA. Best selling author of humorous travel books. Lived and worked in Kirkby Malham for several years. He wrote "I don't know for sure if Malhamdale is the finest place there is until I have died and seen heaven (assuming they let me at least have a glance), but until that day comes it will certainly do."

7. **Janet Street Porter**
   Born 1946 in Brentford, Middlesex. Journalist and TV presenter. She has had a home in upper Nidderdale since 1978. Janet is a keen walker and loves the Yorkshire Dales.

8. **Sebastian Coe**
   Born 1956 in Chiswick, London. 1500m Olympic gold medallist in 1980 and '84. Conservative MP from 1992-97. Head of the London bid to host the 2012 Olympics. Chairman of the London Organising Committee for the Olympic Games. Coe was brought up in Sheffield and joined Hallamshire Harriers aged 12.

9. **Colin Montgomerie**
   Born 1963 in Glasgow. Golfer. 5-time major championship runner-up and ranked as high as number two in the world. He was raised in Yorkshire. His father was managing director of Fox's Biscuits. He was educated at Leeds Grammar School and played golf at Ilkley Golf Club.

10. **Sir Roger Moore**
    Born 1927 in London. He attended Roe Head School in Mirfield.

Others:

Rowan Williams - the Archbishop of Canterbury. Born 1950 in Swansea. Lectured at the College of the Resurrection in Mirfield for two years from 1976.

C-3PO
Anthony Daniels played the droid C-3PO in the *Star Wars* films made between 1977 and 2005. Born 1946 in Salisbury. Attended Giggleswick School near Settle.

Shelley Rudman
Born in Wiltshire in 1981. Now lives in Sheffield. She won a silver medal at the 2006 Winter Olympic Games in the skeleton bob.

Richard Hammond
Born in Solihull 1969. *Top Gear* presenter. Moved to Ripon with his family in the mid-1980s.

James May
Born in Bristol in 1963. *Top Gear* presenter. Spent his teenage years in Rotherham.

Famous former Yorkshire residents not born in Yorkshire (deceased)

1. **Richard III**
   1452-1485. Born at Fotheringhay Castle in Northamptonshire. King of England for two years from 1483-85. Last king of the House of York and of the Plantagenet dynasty. His defeat (and death) at the Battle of Bosworth Field was the decisive battle in the Wars of the Roses. Linked to the legend of the Princes in the Tower, whom he is thought to have murdered. Richard spent several years of his childhood at Middleham Castle in Wensleydale. Shakespeare portrayed Richard as a villain but perhaps he did this to gain favour with the Tudors.

2. **Mary Queen of Scots**
   She was imprisoned at Bolton Castle in Wensleydale from July 1568 to January 1569. She was then imprisoned in Sheffield Castle and Sheffield Manor Lodge until her execution in 1587. Mary had a strong claim to the English

throne and therefore posed a threat to Queen Elizabeth I who was her cousin. Mary's son was King James VI of Scotland. He became king James I of England when Queen Elizabeth died without heir in 1603.

3. **Laurence Stern**
1713-1768. Born in Clonmel, County Tipperary, Ireland. Best known for his novel *The Life and Opinions of Tristram Shandy*. He attended Hipperholme Grammar School. After attending Jesus College, Cambridge, Stern became the vicar of Sutton-on-the-Forest near Easingwold.

4. **William Herschel**
Born 1738 in Hanover, Germany. Astronomer and composer. Most famous for discovering the planet Uranus in 1781. Emigrated to Britain when he was 19.
Herschel lived for a number of years in Halifax where in 1766 he was the first organist of the Parish Church of St. John the Baptist, which since 2009 has been called Halifax Minster.

5. **Sir Robert Peel**
1788-1850. Born in Bury, Lancashire. Prime Minister twice, December 1834 to April 1835 and August 1841 to June 1846. He founded the Metropolitan Police in 1829. The new policemen were called "Bobbies" after Sir Robert. Peel was educated at Hipperholme Grammar School near Halifax from 1798.

6. **Barbara Castle**
1910-2003. Born in Chesterfield but raised in Pontefract and Bradford. One of the most important politicians of the 20th Century. As Minister of Transport from 1965-68 she introduced the breathalyser and made permanent the 70mph speed limit. She also presided over the closure of 2000 miles of railway line as recommended by Beeching.

7. **Alf Wight**
   1916-95. Born in Sunderland and moved to Thirsk in 1940. Wrote his books under the pen name James Herriot.

8. **Philip Larkin**
   1922-85. Born in Coventry. Poet. In 2008 the *Times* named him as the greatest British post-war writer. He lived in Hull from 1955 until his death. He was librarian at the University of Hull.

9. **Russell Harty**
   1934-88. Born in Blackburn, Lancashire. Harty was a TV presenter of arts programmes and chat shows. On leaving Oxford University where he gained a first-class degree in English literature, he became an English and drama teacher at Giggleswick School near Settle. One of his pupils was Richard Whiteley.

10. **John Goodricke**
    1764-86. Born in the Netherlands, but lived much of his life in York. He was an eminent and profoundly deaf amateur astronomer who made some very important discoveries.

Others:

Patrick McGoohan
1928-2009. Born in New York. Parents moved to Sheffield when he was 7. After leaving school he worked as a chicken farmer, a bank clerk and a lorry driver before getting a job as a stage manager at Sheffield Repertory Theatre. When one of the actors became ill McGoohan filled in, launching his acting career. Best known for *The Prisoner*.

SPORT

Sporting world champions

I know it says top ten on the front cover, but it's only fair that I list all twelve of the individual world champions from Yorkshire. If I've missed any out, please let me know. To keep it to twelve I've listed the boxing world champions separately.

1. **Beryl Burton**
   1937-96. Born in the Halton area of Leeds. Cyclist. On the track she was individual pursuit world champion five times in 1959, 60, 62, 63 and 66. Burton was also road race world champion in 1960 and 67.

2. **Sarah Stevenson**
   Born in Doncaster in 1983. Taekwondo world champion in 2001 and 2011.

3. **James Toseland**
   Born in Doncaster in 1980. 2004 and 2007 world superbike champion.

4. **Debbie Flood**
   Born in Harrogate in 1980. World champion in the Women's rowing quadruple skulls in 2006, 2007 and 2010.

5. **Lizzie Armistead**
   Born in Otley in 1988. Track cycling team pursuit world champion in 2009.

6. **Jessica Ennis**
   Born 1986 in Sheffield. World heptathlon champion in 2009.

7. **Paul Goodison**
   Born in Brinsworth near Rotherham in 1977. World
   champion 2009 in laser class sailing.

8. **Alistair Brownlee**
   Born in Dewsbury in 1988. 2009 and 2011 world triathlon
   champion.

9. **Jonathan Brownlee**
   Born in Leeds 1990, brother of Alistair. 2010 and 2011
   sprint triathlon world champion.

10. **Nicholas Matthew**
    Born in Sheffield in 1980. Squash world champion in 2010
    and 2011.

11. **Ed Clancy**
    Born in Barnsley in 1985. 2010 omnium cycling world
    champion. The omnium consists of five events - a sprint
    200m time trial, scratch race, 3 km individual pursuit,
    points race and a 1 km time trial. Ed has also been world
    champion in cycling team pursuit in 2005, 2007 and 2010.

12. **Ben Swift**
    Born in Rotherham in 1987. Won the world championship
    in the scratch race at the 2012 track cycling world
    championship.

Boxing world champions:

Naseem Hamed
Born in Sheffield to Yemeni parents in 1974. World featherweight boxing champion 1995 to 2001.

Paul Jones
Born in Sheffield in 1966. World light middleweight champion in 1995.

Johnny Nelson
Born in Sheffield in 1967. World cruiserweight boxing champion 1999 to 2005.

Paul Ingle
Born in Scarborough in 1972. IBF featherweight world champion in 1999.

Clinton Woods
Born in Sheffield in 1972. World light-heavyweight champion 2005 to 2007.

Junior Witter
Born in Bradford in 1974. WBC light welterweight champion 2006-2008

Are snooker and darts sports? I'm not sure, so I've listed these three separately:

Joe Johnson
Born in Bradford in 1959. Snooker world champion in 1985. This was Joe's only ranking tournament win, although he proved it wasn't a fluke by reaching the world final the following year.

Dennis Priestley

Born in Mexborough in 1950. He was the first player to win both the BDO and WDC (now PDC) world championships, in 1991 and 1994 respectively.

John Walton

Born in Bradford in 1961. Won the BDO world darts championship in 2001.

World champions in team sports are:

Gordon Banks

Born in Sheffield in 1937. Football World Cup winner 1966.

Jason Robinson

Born in Leeds in 1974. Won the rugby union world cup in 2003.

Mike Tindall

Born in Otley in 1978. Also won the 2003 rugby union world cup.

Nicola Jackson

Born in Northallerton in 1984. Swimmer who won gold in the 4 x 200m relay at the world championships in 2000 and 2001.

Debbie Flood

Born in Harrogate in 1980. Rowing women's quads world champion in 2006, 2007 and 2010.

Nicola Minichiello

Born in Sheffield in 1978. The first British female bobsleigh driver to win a world championship in 2009. She did this with Gillian Cooke from Scotland.

Olympic medallists

Yorkshire born athletes had a great Olympics in 2012: five golds (Ed Clancy, Jessica Ennis, Alistair Brownlee, Nicola Adams and Luke Campbell), one silver (Lizzie Armistead) and two bronze (Ed Clancy and Jonny Brownlee). Some parts of the media claimed that Yorkshire had four other medallists (Andy Triggs-Hodge - rowing, Kat Copeland - rowing, Tom Ransley - rowing and Nicola Wilson - team eventing), however, these four were not born in Yorkshire.

There are ten Yorkshire born gold medallists.

1. **Ed Clancy**
   Born in Barnsley in 1985. Two gold medals in cycling team pursuit in 2008 and 2012. Also a bronze medal in the omnium in 2012.

2= **Archibald Stinchcombe**
   Born in Cudworth near Barnsley in 1912. Died 1994. Won gold in the men's ice hockey at the 1936 winter Olympics.

2= **Anita Lonsbrough**
   Born in York in 1941. Won the gold medal in the 200m breaststroke at the 1960 Rome games. BBC Sports Personality of the Year in 1962.

2= **Adrian Moorhouse**
   Born in Bradford in 1964. Gold medal winner in the 100m breaststroke at Seoul 1988.

2= **Paul Goodison**
   Born in Brinsworth near Rotherham in 1977. Won the gold medal in sailing's laser class at the 2008 Beijing games. Also world champion in 2009.

2= Anna Tunnicliffe
Born in Doncaster in 1982. Anna is a sailor who won gold in 2008 in the laser radial class. At the age of 12 she and her family moved to the United States and it's that country she represents.

2= Alistair Brownlee
Born in Dewsbury in 1988. Won the triathlon in 2012.

2= Jess Ennis
Born in Sheffield in 1986. Heptathlon champion 2012.

2= Nicola Adams
Born in Leeds in 1982. Flyweight boxing champion in 2012.

2= Luke Campbell
Born in Hull in 1987. Bantamweight boxing champion in 2012.

Other Olympic medallists:

Debbie Flood
Born in Harrogate in 1980. Won silver in the rowing quadruple skulls in both 2004 and 2008.

Dorothy Hyman
Born in Cudworth near Barnsley in 1941. Won the 100m silver and 200m bronze medals at the 1960 Rome games. Also won relay bronze at the 1964 Tokyo games. BBC Sports Personality of the Year 1963. Britain's best ever female sprinter.

Sheila Sherwood
Born in Sheffield in 1945. Won the silver medal in the long jump at the 1968 Mexico City Olympics. Sheila is married to John Sherwood.

Peter Elliott

Born in Rotherham in 1962. Silver medal winner in the 1500m at Seoul in 1988.

John Whitaker

Born in Huddersfield in 1955. Won silver in the equestrian team event at Los Angeles in 1984.

Michael Whitaker

Born in Huddersfield in 1960. In the same silver medal winning team as older brother John.

Lizzie Armistead

Born in Otley in 1988. Silver in the cycling road race in 2012.

Gordon Pirie

Born in Leeds in 1931. Died 1991. 5000m silver medallist at the 1956 games in Melbourne. BBC Sports Personality of the Year in 1955.

Derek Ibbotson

Born in Huddersfield in 1932. 5000m bronze medallist at the 1956 Melbourne games. His most famous achievement was setting a new world record in the mile in 1957.

John Sherwood

Born in Selby in 1945. Won the bronze medal in the 400m hurdles at the 1968 Mexico City Olympics.

Sarah Stevenson

Born in Doncaster in 1983. Taekwondo bronze medallist at Beijing 2008.

Joanne Jackson

Born in Northallerton in 1986. Bronze medal winner in the 400m freestyle at Beijing in 2008.

Jonny Clay
Born in Leeds in 1963. Won bronze in the cycling team pursuit in Sydney 2000.

Jonny Brownlee
Born in Leeds in 1990. Bronze medal in the triathlon in 2012.

MOST SUCCESSFUL FOOTBALL CLUBS

This is in terms of how many times clubs have been English champions (either of the Premiership or the old First Division). 23 clubs throughout the country have been champions, four of them are from Yorkshire. The other six clubs in this list are ranked in terms of FA Cup wins, then League Cup wins, then best cup performance and lastly best end of season league position.

1. **Sheffield Wednesday** 4 times winners of division 1 (1902-03, 1903-04, 1928-29, 1929-30). Also winners of the FA Cup three times, the last being in 1935.

2= **Leeds United** 3 titles (1968-69, 1973-74, 1991-92). Also winners of the FA Cup once in 1972.

2= **Huddersfield Town** 3 titles (1923-24, 1924-25, 1925-26). Also winners of the FA Cup once in 1922.

4. **Sheffield United** 1 title (1897-98). Also won the FA Cup 4 times, the last win being in 1925.

5= **Barnsley** 1 FA Cup win in 1912.

5= **Bradford City** 1 FA Cup win in 1911

7. **Middlesbrough** 1 League Cup win in 2004

8. **Rotherham Utd** runners-up in the League Cup in 1961

9. **Hull City** finished 17th in The Premiership 2008-09 season. After nine matches of that season they were joint top on points. Just ten years earlier they had been bottom of the fourth tier of English football.

10. **Doncaster Rovers** finished 12th in The Championship (2nd division) in the 2009-10 season.

Oldest league football clubs in Yorkshire

Yorkshire is officially recognised by FIFA as the birth-place of club football. Sheffield FC founded in 1857 is certified as the oldest association football club in the world. The club currently plays in the Northern Premier League Division One South. The club's home is now the Coach and Horses ground at Dronfield in Derbyshire. The world's first inter-club match was between Sheffield FC and Hallam FC in 1860.

1. **Sheffield Wednesday** 1867
2. **Middlesbrough** 1876
3. **Doncaster Rovers** 1879
4. **Barnsley** 1887
5. **Rotherham United** 1888
6. **Sheffield United** 1889
7. **Bradford City** 1903
8. **Hull City** 1904
9. **Huddersfield Town** 1908
10. **Leeds United** 1919

Biggest football grounds

1. **Leeds United** - Elland Road, capacity 40,204
2. **Sheffield Wednesday** - Hillsborough, 39,812
3. **Middlesbrough** - Riverside Stadium, 35,100
4. **Sheffield United** - Bramall Lane, 32,702
5. **Hull City** - KC Stadium, 25,404
6. **Bradford City** - Coral Windows Stadium, 25,136
7. **Huddersfield Town** - Galpharm Stadium, 24,500
8. **Barnsley** - Oakwell, 23,009
9. **Doncaster Rovers** - Keepmoat Stadium, 15,231
10. **Rotherham United** - New York Stadium, 12,021

Greatest footballers

1. **Gordon Banks**
   Born in Sheffield in 1937. 1966 World Cup winner as goalkeeper. The International Federation of Football History and Statistics named Banks as the second greatest goalkeeper of all time behind Lev Yashin. Played for Chesterfield, Leicestershire City and Stoke City. Played 73 times for England between 1963 and 1972.

2. **Kevin Keegan**
   Born in Armthorpe near Doncaster in 1951. Played for Scunthorpe United, Liverpool, Hamburg, Southampton and Newcastle United. He also played for England 63 times (scoring 21 goals) from 1972 to 1982. Keegan was European footballer of the year in 1978 and '79.

3. **David Seaman**
   Born in Rotherham in 1963. Played a total of 731 games for Peterborough United, Birmingham City, Queen's Park Rangers, Arsenal and Manchester City. Seaman also played 75 times for England.

4. Wilf Mannion

1918-2000. Born in South Bank near Middlesbrough. Played as an inside forward and scored 99 goals in 341 appearances for Middlesbrough. Played 26 times and scored 11 goals for England between 1946 and 51.

5. Ron Flowers

Born in Edington, Doncaster in 1934. Midfielder, played for Wolves from 1952-67 and also for England 1955-66. Ron played 49 times for England and scored ten goals. He was a member of the victorious 1966 World Cup squad, though he never kicked a ball during the tournament.

6. George Hardwick

1920-2004. Born in Saltburn. Fullback for Middlesbrough. He is widely regarded as the club's greatest ever defender. Played 13 times for England and was his country's first post WW2 captain. His international career was cut short by injury.

7. Brian Clough

Born in Middlesbrough in 1935. Died 2004.
Played for Middlesbrough and then Sunderland. In 274 appearances for both clubs he scored a remarkable 251 goals. Played twice for England in 1959 but failed to score. He suffered a cruciate ligament injury in 1962 which ended his career. For players having scored over 200 English league goals, he has the highest goals per game ratio of 0.916.

8. Len Shackleton

Born in Bradford in 1922. Died 2000. He was known as The Clown Prince of Football and is one of football's greatest ever entertainers. Played for Bradford Park Avenue, Newcastle United and Sunderland. He scored 297 goals in 622 games. He also played five times for England and scored once.

9. **Trevor Cherry**

Born in Huddersfield in 1948. Played for Huddersfield Town, Leeds United and Bradford City. He also played 27 times for England, captaining the side once.

Cherry is the only England player to be sent off in a friendly. It was against Argentina in 1977. He lost two teeth after being punched in the mouth by Daniel Bertoni, who Cherry had brought down with a nasty tackle from behind. Bertoni was also red-carded.

10. **Paul Madeley**

Born in Leeds in 1944. Played 536 games for Leeds United and 24 for England. In a 17 year career at Leeds he played in every position on the pitch, except goalkeeper, and wore every shirt number from two to 11. Madeley's record as a utility player remains unique in English football.

And also:

David Pegg

Born in Doncaster in 1935. David was one of the eight Manchester United players who lost their lives in the Munich air disaster on 6th February 1958. He played 127 times for United and once for England.

Ebenezer Cobb Morley

Born in Hull in 1831. Although his name is all but forgotten, Morley is arguably one of the most influential men in sporting history. He was a lawyer and enjoyed playing football. At the time teams played by different rules, playing one team's version in each half. Morley believed that the game needed common rules and a governing body. In 1862 he became a founding member of the F.A. In 1863 he chaired a group that drew up the rules we know today, thus the modern game was born.

Best footballers of the last 20 years

1. **David Seaman**
   Born in Rotherham in 1963. Played a total of 731 games for Peterborough United, Birmingham City, Queen's Park Rangers, Arsenal and Manchester City. Seaman also played 75 times for England.

2. **David Batty**
   Born in Leeds in 1968. Played for Leeds, Blackburn and Newcastle. Also won 42 England caps.

3. **Paul Robinson**
   Born in Beverley in 1979. Played for Leeds, Spurs and Blackburn. 41 England caps.

4. **James Milner**
   Born in Leeds in 1986. Has played for Leeds United, Swindon Town, Newcastle United, Aston Villa and currently for Manchester City. 24 England caps as of April 2012.

5. **Nick Barmby**
   Born in Hull in 1974. Played for Spurs, Middlesbrough, Everton, Liverpool, Leeds, Nottingham Forest and Hull. 23 England caps.

6. **Aaron Lennon**
   Born in Leeds in 1987. Has played for Leeds United and currently for Tottenham Hotspur. 19 England caps as of April 2012.

7. **Alan Smith**
   Born in Rothwell in 1980. Has played for Leeds, Manchester United, Newcastle and MK Dons. Also 19 caps for England.

8. **Gary Cahill**
   Born in Sheffield in 1985. Has played for Aston Villa, Derby County and Chelsea. Currently nine England caps.

9. **Jonathan Woodgate**
   Born in Middlesbrough in 1980. Has played for Leeds, Newcastle, Real Madrid, Middlesbrough, Spurs and Stoke. Eight England caps.

10. **Brian Deane**
    Born in Leeds in 1968. Played for nine football clubs - Doncaster Rovers, Sheffield United, Leeds United, Benfica, Middlesbrough, Leicester City, West Ham, Sunderland and Perth Glory. Three England caps.

Football Managers

1. **Brian Clough**
   Born in Middlesbrough in 1935. Died 2004. Widely considered to be one of the greatest managers of all time and the greatest to have never managed England. In five years he took Derby from the foot of division 2 to first division champions in 1972. Later in the 1970s he did pretty much the same with Nottingham Forest. They won the first division in 1978. In 1979 and 1980 Forest won the European Cup. Clough was the first manager to win the first division with two clubs since Herbert Chapman.

2. **Herbert Chapman**
   Born in Kiverton Park near Rotherham in 1878. Died in 1934. Managed Northampton Town and Leeds City prior to World War 1. After the war he managed Huddersfield

Town and won an F.A. Cup and two first division titles. In 1925 he moved to Arsenal, again winning an F.A. Cup and two first division titles. He set Arsenal up to be the dominant team of the 1930s, although he didn't see it, dying suddenly in 1934 from pneumonia.

Chapman was regarded as one of football's first modernisers. He developed new tactics and training methods and championed innovations such as numbered shirts, European competitions and floodlighting.

3. **Don Revie**
Born in Middlesbrough in 1927. Died in 1989 of motor neurone disease.

He managed Leeds United from 1961 to 1974 when he resigned to take over as England manager. With Leeds he won the first division twice in 1969 and '74. He also won the European Fairs Cup in 1968 and the F.A. Cup in 1972. Leeds were also runners-up in the league championship in 1965, '66, '70 and '71 and runners-up in the F.A. Cup in '65 and '73.

4. **Bill Nicholson**
Born in Scarborough in 1919. Died in 2004. Bill devoted his life to Tottenham Hotspur. He played for the club from 1938 to 1955 and managed them from 1958 to 1974. His time in charge of Spurs was the most successful period in the club's history. In 1961 they won the first "double" of the twentieth century. The following year they won the FA Cup again, and narrowly missed a place in the European Cup Final, losing to Benfica in the semi-final. In the 1962-63 season, Nicholson put Spurs in the history books once again when they became the first British club to win a major European trophy. On May 15th 1963, in Rotterdam, Spurs defeated Atlético Madrid 5-1 to win the European Cup Winners Cup.

In 1967 Spurs won their third FA Cup in seven years.

This was followed by the League Cup in 1971 and 1973 and the UEFA Cup in 1972. Bill resigned as manager of Spurs in August 1974, shortly after Spurs had lost the 1974 UEFA Cup final to Feyenoord.

5. George Raynor

Born in Wombwell, Barnsley in 1907. Died 1985. Alf Ramsey is not the only English manager to take a side to the World Cup final. George Raynor did it with Sweden in 1958. His side was beaten 5-2 by a Pele inspired Brazil. Eight years earlier he had taken Sweden to the semi-finals where they were beaten by eventual winners Uruguay.

After leaving Sweden, George was expected to have no shortage of offers of work in England. However, he was ignored by the top clubs and so went to work with Midland League part-timers Skegness. He supplemented his wage by working as a storeman at the local Butlins holiday camp. In the 1967-68 season he had a seven month stint managing fourth division Doncaster Rovers.

George Raynor passed away in 1985, aged 78. His death went unrecorded in English newspapers.

6. Howard Wilkinson

Born in Sheffield in 1943. He managed Leeds United from 1988 to '96 and won the first division championship in 1992, the final season before the creation of the Premiership. Wilkinson is the last English-born manager to win the English league championship.

7. Kevin Keegan

Born in Armthorpe near Doncaster in 1961. Managed Newcastle United to second place in the Premiership in 1996. Keegan managed England from 1999 to 2000.

8. **Steve McClaren**
Born in Fulford near York in 1961. Managed Middlesbrough between 2001 and 2006 and won the League Cup in 2004. This was the club's first major trophy. McClaren went on to manage England in 2006 and 2007. Perhaps he will always be remembered as "the wally with the brolly".

9. **Mick McCarthy**
Born in Barnsley in 1959. He's managed Millwall, Ireland, Sunderland and Wolves. McCarthy managed Ireland from 1996 to 2002, taking them to the second round of the World Cup in 2002, where they were knocked out by Spain in a penalty shoot-out.

10. **Neil Warnock**
Born in Sheffield in 1948. Warnock has managed several clubs, including Sheffield United from 1999 to 2007. In 2003 he took The Blades to the semi-finals of the League Cup and F.A. Cup. In 2005 the club gained promotion to the Premiership as runners-up in the Championship. In 2010 Warnock took over at QPR and in 2011 saw them promoted as champions from the Championship. Sacked by QPR in 2012 he then took over at Leeds United.

Bill Shankly
Did you know that before becoming manager of Liverpool he managed Huddersfield Town from 1956-59?

GREATEST QUOTES BY BRIAN CLOUGH

1. "I wouldn't say I was the best manager, but I was in the top one."
2. "It only takes a second to score a goal."
3. (Reflecting on England's exit from Euro 2000) "Players lose you games, not tactics. There's so much crap talked about tactics by people who barely know how to win at dominoes."
4. (On dealing with a player who disagrees with him) "We talk about it for twenty minutes and then we decide I was right."
5. (On getting things done) "Rome wasn't built in a day, but I wasn't on that particular job."
6. (On the importance of passing to feet) "If God had wanted us to play football in the clouds, he'd have put grass up there."
7. (On explaining his nickname) "On occasions I have been big headed. I think most people are when they get in the limelight. I call myself Big Head just to remind myself not to be."
8. "The ugliest player I ever signed was Kenny Burns." A Clough compliment for one of his most talented players.
9. "Take your hands out of your pockets." Advice for a young Trevor Francis as he receives an award from his manager.
10. "For all his horses, knighthoods and championships, he hasn't got two of what I've got. And I don't mean balls!" Referring to Sir Alex Ferguson's failure to win two successive European Cups.

What Bill Shankly once said about Cloughie:

"He's worse than the rain in Manchester. At least the rain in Manchester stops occasionally."

GREATEST EVER PLAYERS FOR LEEDS UNITED

Compiled in 2000 by Leeds United

1. **Billy Bremner**
2. **John Charles**
3. **Eddie Gray**
4. **Bobby Collins**
5. **Allan Clarke**
6. **Jack Charlton**
7. **Norman Hunter**
8. **Paul Reaney**
9. **Peter Lorimer**
10. **Mick Jones**

HIGHEST EVER SCORERS FOR LEEDS UNITED

1. **Peter Lorimer** 238
2. **John Charles** 157
3. **Allan Clarke** 151
4. **Tom Jennings** 117
5. **Billy Bremner** 115
6. **Johnny Giles** 114
7. **Mick Jones** 111
8. **Charlie Keetley** 110
9. **Jack Charlton** 95
10. **Russell Wainscoat** 93

Most appearances for Leeds United

1= **Jack Charlton** 773 (1952-73)
1= **Billy Bremner** 773 (1959-76)
3. **Paul Reaney** 745 (1962-78)
4= **Paul Madeley** 724 (1963-80)
4= **Norman Hunter** 724 (1962-76)
6. **Peter Lorimer** 703 (1962-79 and 84-85) (made his debut at the age of 15 - a club record)
7. **Eddie Gray** 577 (1965-83)
8. **Gary Kelly** 531 (1992-2007)
9. **Johnny Giles** 525 (1963-75)
10. **Gary Sprake** 506 (1962-73)

Highest ever scorers for Sheffield Wednesday

1. **Andrew Wilson** 217
2. **John Fantham** 167
3= **David Hirst** 149
3= **Redfern Froggatt** 149
5. **Ellis Rimmer** 140
6. **Mark Hooper** 136
7= **Fred Spiksley** 114
7= **Jimmy Trotter** 114
9. **David McLean** 100
10. **Harry Chapman** 99

Most appearances for Sheffield Wednesday

1. **Andrew Wilson** 560 (1900-20)
2. **Jack Brown** 507 (1922-37)
3. **Alan Finney** 503 (1949-65)
4. **Kevin Pressman** 478 (1985-2004)
5. **Tommy Crawshaw** 465 (1894-1908)
6. **Redfern Froggatt** 458 (1942-60)
7. **Don Megson** 442 (1952-70)
8. **John Fantham** 435 (1956-1969)
9= **Ernest Blenkinsop** 424 (1923-1934)
9= **Teddy Davison** 424 (1908-26)

Highest ever scorers for Sheffield United

1. **Harry Johnson** 252
2. **Alan Woodward** 193
3. **Doc Pace** 175
4. **Keith Edwards** 170
5. **Jimmy Dunne** 167
6. **Jimmy Hagan** 151
7. **Billy Gillespie** 142
8. **Fred Tunstall** 135
9= **Jack Pickering** 119
9= **Brian Deane** 119

MOST APPEARANCES FOR SHEFFIELD UNITED

1. **Joe Shaw** 713 (1945-66)
2. **Alan Hodgkinson** 674 (1954-71)
3. **Alan Woodward** 640 (1964-78)
4. **Ernest Needham** 544 (1891-1910)
5. **Len Badger** 543 (1962-76)
6. **Billy Gillespie** 507 (1911-31)
7. **Graham Shaw** 497 (1952-67)
8. **Fred Tunstall** 491 (1920-32)
9. **Cec Coldwell** 475 (1952-66)
10. **George Green** 438 (1923-34)

GREATEST CRICKETERS

1. **Sir Len Hutton**
   Born in Pudsey in 1916. Died 1990. Perhaps England's finest post-war batsman. Played in 79 Test matches, averaging 56.67.

2. **Fred Trueman**
   Born in Stainton near Doncaster in 1931. Died in 2006. Fiery Fred is one of the greatest fast bowlers in history. Played in 67 Tests and took 307 wickets with a bowling average of 21.57. He was the first person in history to take 300 Test wickets.

3. **Geoffrey Boycott**
   Born in Fitzwilliam near Wakefield in 1940. Boycott was an opening batsman. He played in 108 Tests and scored a total of 8114 runs. His Test batting average was 47.72.

4. **Brian Close**

   Born in Rawdon near Leeds in 1931. He is the youngest man ever to play Test cricket for England. In 1949 he was picked to play against New Zealand when only 18 years old. Close played 22 Tests for England, seven as captain.

5. **Ray Illingworth**

   Born in Pudsey in 1932. Played in 61 Tests, 31 as captain. Under Illingworth England won the Ashes in 1971 and 1972.

6. **Wilfred Rhodes**

   Born in Kirkheaton near Huddersfield in 1877. Died 1973. He holds the world records for the most matches played in first-class cricket (1,110) and for the most wickets taken (4,204). He completed the double of 1,000 runs and 100 wickets in an English county cricket season a record 16 times. In his 58 Test matches for England he took 127 wickets and scored 2,325 runs. He was the first Englishman to achieve the double of 100 Test wickets and 1,000 Test runs. In his final Test in 1930 he was 52 years and 165 days old. He is the oldest player to appear in a Test match.

7. **Hedley Verity**

   Born in Headingley in 1905. Died in 1943 from a gunshot wound whilst fighting in Italy during World War 2. He played in 40 Tests for England and in one Test against Australia at Lord's he took 15 wickets. In a county match against Nottingham in 1932 he took ten wickets for ten runs. This remains a world record.

8. **Herbert Sutcliffe**

   Born in Summerbridge near Pateley Bridge in 1894. Died 1978. Opening batsman who played in 54 Test matches with a batting average of 60.73. This is the highest average of any English batsman.

9. **Jim Laker**

Born in Frizinghall in Bradford in 1922. Died 1986. Brought up in Saltaire by his aunts, his plans to play for Yorkshire were ended by the outbreak of the Second World War. In 1945 Laker settled in Surrey, where he played his cricket. He therefore never played for Yorkshire. Between 1948 and 1959 he played in 46 Tests and had a bowling average of 21.24.

10. **Chris Old**

Born in Middlesbrough in 1948. Played in 46 Tests from 1972 to 1981. He was a right arm swing bowler and powerful late order left handed batter. Mike Brearley, his England captain, described him as a talent to rival Ian Botham. Old hit the third fastest century of all time in 1977 at Edgbaston. His 100 came off 72 balls in 37 minutes.

Dickie Bird

Born 1933 in Barnsley. We all know Dickie as the great cricket umpire, but he also played professionally for Yorkshire and Leicestershire as a batsman from 1956 to 1964. As a young man he played club cricket in the same team as Geoff Boycott and Michael Parkinson.

Thomas Lord. Heard of him? In a way you have. Born in Thirsk in 1755, died in 1832. He is best remembered as the founder of Lord's Cricket Ground.

QUOTES BY SIR LEN HUTTON

"In an England cricket eleven, the flesh may be of the South, but the bone is of the North, and the backbone is Yorkshire."

"Ladies playing cricket - absurd. Just like a man trying to knit."

"If my mother hadn't thrown my football boots on the fire, I might have become as famous as Denis Compton."

"Whenever I saw Wally Hammond batting, I felt sorry for the ball."

Most runs for Yorkshire

1. **Herbert Sutcliffe** 38,558 (played for Yorkshire 1919-45)
2. **David Denton** 33,282 (1894-1920)
3. **Geoffrey Boycott** 32,570 (1962-86)
4. **George Hirst** 32,035 (1891-1929)
5. **Wilfred Rhodes** 31,098 (1898-1930)
6. **Percy Holmes** 26,220 (1913-33)
7. **Morris Leyland** 26,181 (1920-46)
8. **Sir Len Hutton** 24,807 (1934-55)
9. **Brian Close** 22,650 (1949-70)
10. **John Hampshire** 21,979 (1961-81)

Most wickets for Yorkshire

1. **Wilfred Rhodes** 3597 (played for Yorkshire 1898-1930)
2. **George Hirst** 2477 (1891-1929)
3. **Schofield Haigh** 1876 (1895-1913)
4. **George Macaulay** 1774 (1920-35)
5. **Fred Trueman** 1745 (1949-68)
6. **Hedley Verity** 1558 (1930-39)
7. **Johnny Wardle** 1539 (1946-58)
8. **Ray Illingworth** 1431 (1951-83)
9. **Bill Bowes** 1351 (1929-47)
10. **Bobby Peel** 1330 (1882-97)

LONGEST SERVING CRICKET CAPTAINS

Yorkshire County Cricket Club was founded in 1863. As of 2012 there have been 35 captains.

1. **Lord Hawke** 27 years (1883-1910, champions 8 times)
2. **Brian Sellers** 14 years (1933-47, champions 6 times)
3. **Roger Iddison** 9 years (1863-72, champions 3 times)
4= **Norman Yardley** 7 years (1948-55, champions once)
4= **Brian Close** 7 years (1963-70, champions 4 times)
4= **Geoff Boycott** 7 years (1971-78)
7. **Archibald White** 6 years (1912-18, champions once)
8. **Martyn Moxon** 5 years (1990-95)
9. **David Byas** 5 years (1996-2001, champions once)
10. **Tom Emmett** 4 years (1878-82)

MOST RUGBY LEAGUE TITLES

Rugby league developed after the great schism of 1895. Up until 1895 there was one national rugby competition run by the Rugby Union. Some northern rugby clubs wanted to allow payments to players to compensate them for loss of earnings; rugby was of course amateur at the time and such payments were not allowed. This resulted in the great split. On August 29, at the George Hotel in Huddersfield, the Northern Rugby Football Union (NRFU) was officially announced. It was made up from 22 of the leading clubs from Yorkshire and Lancashire. The NRFU became known as Rugby League in 1922.

From 1895 to 1908 major changes were made to the game by the NRFU that made rugby league quite different to rugby union.

The first matches of the Northern Union were played on 7 September 1895. In 1896, Manningham were the first champions. From 1896-1901 the league was split in two. There was a Yorkshire League and a Lancashire League. In 1901 the top clubs from each league resigned to form a single new league. Broughton Rangers were the first champions. In the following season the remaining clubs from the two counties formed a second division.

In the 1896/7 season the Northern Union introduced a challenge cup open to all teams in Yorkshire and Lancashire. In the first final, played at Headingley, in front of 14,000 fans, Batley beat St. Helens 10-3.

The Rugby Football League Championship was superseded by the Super League in 1996. Both titles are counted below.

1. **Leeds** 9 (last win 2012)
2. **Huddersfield** 7 (last win 61-62)
3= **Hull** 6 (82-83)
3= **Bradford Bulls** 6 (2005)
5. **Hull KR** 5 (84-85)
6. **Halifax** 4 (85-86)
7= **Wakefield Trinity** 2 (67-68)
7= **Hunslet** 2 (37-38)
9= **Featherstone Rovers** 1 (76-77)
9= **Dewsbury** 1 (72-73)
9= **Batley** 1 (23-24)
9= **Bradford FC** 1 (1903-04) In 1907 Bradford FC stopped playing rugby and switched to association football. Some members left the club and set up a new rugby club called Bradford Northern, now known as Bradford Bulls.
9= **Manningham** 1 (1895-96) They were the first winners of the new Northern League.

Wigan have won the most titles (19), St. Helens are second (12) and Leeds are third.

Most Challenge Cup wins

1. **Leeds** 11 (last win 1999)
2. **Huddersfield** 6 (1953)
3. **Halifax** 5 (1987)
4. **Bradford Bulls** 5 (2003)
5. **Wakefield Trinity** 5 (1963)
6. **Castleford** 4 (1986)
7. **Hull** 3 (2005)
8. **Featherstone Rovers** 3 (1983)
9. **Batley** 3 (1901)
10= **Dewsbury** 2 (1943)
10= **Hunslet** 2 (1934)

Wigan have the most wins (18), St.Helens are second (12 wins) and Leeds are third.

Biggest rugby league stadiums

1. **Sheffield Eagles Bramall Lane**, 32,700 capacity
2. **Hull FC KC Stadium** 25,404
3. **Galpharm Stadium Huddersfield Giants** 24,500
4. **Headingley Stadium Leeds Rhinos** 20,500
5. **Odsal Stadium home** of **Bradford Bulls** 20,000
6. **Keepmoat Stadium Doncaster Rugby League Club** 15,200
7. **Shay Stadium Halifax** 14,000
8. **The PROBIZ Colliseum**, Wheldon Road, **Castleford Tigers** 11,750
   In 2012 **Castleford** will move to a new 13,000 seat stadium.
9. **Belle Vue Stadium** (The Rapid Solicitors Stadium) **Wakefield Wildcats** 12,000
10. **Hull KR New Craven Park** 10,000

Racecourses

Yorkshire has nine top class racecourses - more than any other region in the UK. There are six flat racing courses at York, Beverley, Pontefract, Redcar, Ripon and Thirsk, a specialist National Hunt course at Wetherby and dual courses offering racing on the flat or over jumps at Catterick and Doncaster.

The courses are ranked in order of the number of race days in 2011.

1. **Doncaster** (34)
2. **Catterick** (27)
3. **Beverley** (20)
4. **Redcar** (18)
5= **Wetherby** (17)
5= **York** (17)
7. **Pontefract** (16)
8. **Ripon** (15)
9. **Thirsk** (13)
10. **Kiplingcotes** - a small hamlet near Market Weighton. It's home to the Kiplingcotes Derby - the country's oldest flat race, dating back to 1519.

CITIES, TOWNS
AND VILLAGES

LARGEST CITIES AND TOWNS IN YORKSHIRE

There's much confusion about the status of places in the far north of the county due to the governmental changes made in the 1970s. However, in 1996 the river Tees was re-established as the border between North Yorkshire and County Durham for ceremonial purposes only. Thus, Middlesbrough, Redcar and Cleveland and Stockton-on-Tees south of the river are part of the ceremonial county of North Yorkshire.

Figures for population are mostly from the 2001 census. Figures are also for the actual cities and towns and not the wider metropolitan boroughs.

1. **Leeds** (population 715,404) It's the third biggest city in England behind London and Birmingham.
2. **Sheffield** (513,100)
3. **Bradford** (293,717)
4. **Kingston-upon-Hull** (243,589)
5. **Huddersfield** (146,234) 10th largest town in UK
6. **Middlesbrough** (142,400)*
7. **York** (137,505)
8. **Rotherham** (117,262)
9. **Halifax** (82,056)
10. **Wakefield** (76,886)

* As mentioned above, there's a lot of confusion surrounding places like Middlesbrough; is it in Yorkshire or isn't it? It was historically part of the North Riding of Yorkshire but in 1968 it became part of the County Borough of Teesside and then in 1974 part of the non-metropolitan county of Cleveland. In 1996 Cleveland was abolished and Middlesbrough became a unitary authority within the ceremonial county of North Yorkshire. I hope that clears things up!
Stockton-on-Tees? This town has a population of 83,490. It's the major town in the unitary authority and borough of

Stockton-on-Tees. For ceremonial purposes the borough is split between County Durham (north of the river Tees) and North Yorkshire (south of the river Tees).

LARGEST CITIES/TOWNS IN NORTH YORKSHIRE

1. **Middlesbrough** (142,400)
2. **York** (137,505)
3. **Harrogate** (71,594)
4. **Scarborough** (50,135)
5. **Redcar** (36,610)
6. **Guisborough** (18,108)
7. **Ripon** (15,922)
8. **Northallerton** (15,741)
9. **Knaresborough** (14,740)
10. **Skipton** (14,313)

LARGEST CITIES/TOWNS IN WEST YORKSHIRE

1. **Leeds** (population 715,404)
2. **Bradford** (293,717)
3. **Huddersfield** (146,234)
4. **Halifax** (82,056)
5. **Wakefield** (76,886)
6. **Dewsbury** (54,341)
7. **Keighley** (51,429)
8. **Batley** (49,448)
9. **Castleford** (37,525)
10. **Pudsey** (32 391)

Largest cities/towns in South Yorkshire

1. **Sheffield** (513,100)
2. **Rotherham** (117,262)
3. **Barnsley** (73,500)
4. **Doncaster** (67,977)
5. **Bentley** (33,968)
6. **Anston-Dinnington** (19,086)
7. **Rawmarsh** (18,210)
8. **Maltby** (17,247)
9. **Wath upon Dearne** (16,787)
10. **Thorne-Moorends** (16,592)

Largest cities/towns in East Yorkshire

1. **Kingston-upon-Hull** (243,589)
2. **Bridlington** (33,837)
3. **Beverley** (29,110)
4. **Goole** (17,600)
5. **Cottingham** (17,263)
6. **Hessle** (14,767)
7. **Driffield** (11,477)
8. **Anlaby with Anlaby Common** (9,883)
9. **Hornsea** (8,243)
10. **Willerby** (8,056)

Largest seaside towns

1. **Scarborough** (50,135)
2. **Redcar** (36,610) *
3. **Bridlington** (33,837)
4. **Whitby** (13,594)
5. **Hornsea** (8,243)
6. **Filey** (6,819)
7. **Withernsea** (5,980)
8. **Saltburn-by-the-Sea** (5,912) *
9. **Scalby** 3,953 (?)
10. **Flamborough** (2,121)

   * Redcar and Saltburn-by-the-Sea are part of the unitary authority of Redcar and Cleveland but part of the ceremonial county of North Yorkshire.

Highest villages

This is a list of villages and does not include hamlets. But what's the difference between a hamlet and a village? A hamlet is a group of houses that doesn't contain a church. Villages have churches, or in some cases, once had churches. For heights above-sea-level I've looked at the highest part of each village.

1. **Greenhow** 400m. Near Pateley Bridge in Nidderdale
2. **Queensbury** 360m. Between Bradford and Halifax
3= **Stalling Busk** 330m. Near Semer Water in Wensleydale
3= **Keld** 330m. In Upper Swaledale
5= **Wainstalls** 320m. Near Halifax
6. **Holme** 310m. Near Holmfirth. Pub and school but no church
7= **Oxenhope** 300m. In Airedale near Keighley
7= **Illingworth** 300m. Near Halifax

9= **Middlesmoor** 290m. At the head of Nidderdale
9= **Mixenden** 290m. In Calderdale near Halifax

The far western part of Halifax reaches a height of 325m. Because Halifax is a town I've not included it in the above list.

The highest village in Britain is Flash in Staffordshire. It is 463m above sea-level.

Most scenic market towns in North Yorkshire

Market days shown in brackets.

1. **Hawes** (Tuesday)
2. **Settle** (Tuesday with a farmers' market on the 2nd Sunday of the month)
3. **Helmsley** (Friday)
4. **Leyburn** (Friday with a farmers' market on the 4th Saturday of the month)
5. **Reeth** (Friday)
6. **Richmond** (Saturday with a farmers' market on the 3rd Saturday of the month)
7. **Masham** (Wednesday and Saturday)
8. **Bedale** (Tuesday)
9. **Ripon** (Thursday with a farmers' market on the 3rd Sunday of the month)
10. **Skipton** (Monday, Wednesday, Friday, Saturday with a farmers' market on the 1st Sunday of the month)

Prettiest villages

1. **Burnsall** (in Wharfedale)
2. **Coxwold** (18 miles north of York)
3. **Hutton-le-Hole** (7 miles north-west of Pickering)
4. **Wentworth** (near Rotherham)
5. **Appletreewick** (1 mile from Burnsall)
6. **Reeth** (in Swaledale)
7. **Helmsley** (in the North York Moors midway between Thirsk and Pickering)
8. **Thornton-le-Dale** (2 miles east of Pickering)
9. **Hovingham** (7 miles west of Malton on the edge of the Howardian Hills)
10. **Lealholm** (10 miles north west of Whitby)

Social deprivation

There are 21 local authorities in Yorkshire. They are:

Leeds CC	City of Wakefield MDC
Kirklees	City of Bradford MDC
Calderdale MBC	Sheffield CC
Rotherham MBC	Doncaster MBC
Barnsley MBC	York CC
Selby DC	Scarborough BC
Ryedale DC	Richmondshire DC
Harrogate BC	Craven DC
Kingston-upon-Hull CC	East Riding of Yorkshire Council
Middlesbrough BC	Redcar and Cleveland
Hambleton DC	

(Hambleton DC, Ryedale DC, Harrogate DC, Selby DC, Craven DC, Scarborough BC and Richmondshire DC collectively fall within North Yorkshire County Council.)

Based on the indices of deprivation 2007. This is a deprivation index created by the Department for Communities and Local Government.
The most deprived council districts are:

1. **Kingston-upon-Hull** (11th most deprived district in England)
2. **Bradford** (32nd in England)
3. **Doncaster** (41st)
4. **Barnsley** (43rd)
5. **Sheffield** (63rd)
6. **Wakefield** (66th)
7. **Rotherham** (68th)
8. **Kirklees** (82nd)
9. **Leeds** (85th)
10. **Scarborough** (97th)

The least deprived council districts are, in descending order, Harrogate, Hambleton, Richmondshire, Craven and Selby.

LOCAL AUTHORITIES WITH THE LARGEST POPULATIONS

1. **Leeds** 715,402
2. **Sheffield** 513,234
3. **Bradford** 467,665
4. **Kirklees** 388,567
5. **Wakefield** 315,172
6. **East Riding of Yorkshire Council** 314,113
7. **Doncaster** 286,866
8. **Rotherham** 248,175
9. **Kingston-upon-Hull** 243,589
10. **Barnsley** 218,063

Populations are from the 2001 census

LOCAL AUTHORITIES WITH THE HIGHEST POPULATION DENSITIES

Figures are the number of people per hectare and are from the 2001 census.

1. **Kingston-upon-Hull** 34.09
2. **Middlesbrough** 25.03
3. **Sheffield** 13.95
4. **Leeds** 12.97
5. **Bradford** 12.76
6. **Kirklees** 9.5
7. **Wakefield** 9.31
8. **Rotherham** 8.66
9. **York** 6.66
10. **Barnsley** 6.63

LOCAL AUTHORITIES WITH THE LARGEST MUSLIM POPULATIONS

Figures are percentages of total population and are from the 2001 census.

1. **Bradford** 16.08%
2. **Kirklees** 10.12%
3. **Calderdale** 5.3%
4. **Sheffield** 4.64%
5. **Middlesbrough** 4.22%
6. **Leeds** 2.99%
7. **Rotherham** 2.18%
8. **Wakefield** 1.14%
9. **Kingston-upon-Hull** 0.87%
10. **Doncaster** 0.74%

Settlements with the longest names

1. **Sutton-under-Whitestonecliffe** (27 letters)
2. **Bramham cum Oglethorpe** (20), normally just called Bramham
3= **Middleton on the Wolds** (19)
3= **Holme-on-Spalding-Moor** (19)
3= **Laughton-en-le-Morthen** (19)
6= **Burley-in-Wharfedale** (18)
6= **Thornton in Lonsdale** (18)
8= **Newton upon Derwent** (17)
8= **Sutton upon Derwent** (17)
8= **Sutton-on-the-Forest** (17)

Oddest place names

1. **Booze** - hamlet in the hills above Langthwaite, which is in Arkengarthdale, a tributary valley of Swaledale.
2. **Aike** - village in the East Riding, approximately four miles north of Beverley.
3. **Catfoss** - hamlet in the East Riding, approximately four miles west of Hornsea.
4. **Fangfoss** - village 11 miles east of York.
5. **Nunburnholme** - village three miles east of Pocklington.
6. **Grewelthorpe** - village six miles north of Ripon. Nearby Hackfall is well worth a visit.
7. **Spittal** - hamlet just south of Fangfoss.
8. **Wetwang** - village six miles east of Driffield. Apparently the name means moist penis. The village's honorary mayor was Richard Whiteley and is now Paul Hudson.
9. **Sexhow** - hamlet four miles west of Stokesley.
10. **Bedlam** - small village north of Harrogate.

Other strange place names are Giggleswick, Blubberhouses, Muker, Bugthorpe, Jump, Wressle, Huggate and Warthill.

Places that are in Yorkshire and also outside Yorkshire

1. **Coniston** - there are Conistons north of Hull and north of Grassington and of course in the Lake District.
2. **Easington** - village near Spurn Head. Site of the Easington Gas Terminal which is one of three main gas terminals in the UK. There are also Easingtons in Aberdeenshire, Norfolk and Durham.
3. **Melbourne** - village eight miles west of Market Weighton. Of course, there's also Melbourne in Australia.
4. **Newport** - village seven miles east of Howden in East Yorkshire. Newport is also a city in south Wales.
5. **Preston** - village six miles east of Hull. Also a large town in Lancashire.
6. **Stamford Bridge** - village seven miles east of York. Stamford Bridge is also a football stadium, home to Chelsea.
7. **Richmond** - town in Swaledale and also a town in southwest London. It's also the capital city in the state of Virginia in the USA.
8. **Wales** - a village near Rotherham and also a country. The name Wales has a Germanic root meaning stranger. It suggests that there was a continued Celtic presence in the settlement following the arrival of the anglo-saxons in the 6th Century.
9. **Wentworth** - a village near Rotherham, well known for Wentworth Castle. There's also the Wentworth Estate in Surrey, home to the world famous Wentworth Golf Club.
10. **Halifax** - town in West Yorkshire and also a city in Nova Scotia, Canada.

Most expensive streets to live in

1. **Fulwith Mill Lane**, Harrogate HG2, Average house price £1,225,800
2. **Sandmoor Drive**, Leeds LS17, £1,061,800
3. **Ling Lane**, Scarcroft LS14, £1,047,400
4. **Swindon Lane**, Kirkby Overblow HG3, £1,016,900
5. **Manor House Lane**, Leeds LS17, £1,016,800
6. **Hebers Ghyll Drive**, Ilkley LS29, £979,200
7. **Throstle Nest Drive**, Harrogate HG2, £978,000
8. **Bracken Park**, Scarcroft LS14, £936,700
9. **Alwoodley Gates**, Leeds LS17, £934,900
10. **Tibgarth, Linton** LS22, £915,400

From www.mouseprice.com 2011

Tallest buildings

1. **Bridgewater Place, Leeds** 367 feet. 34th tallest building in the UK. Commonly referred to as the "Dalek".
2. **Sky Plaza, Leeds**. The world's second tallest student accommodation building at 338 feet.
3. **St. Paul's Tower, Sheffield** 331 feet.
4. **Opal Tower, Leeds** 269 feet.
5. **West Riding House, Leeds** 262 feet.
6. **Arts Tower, Sheffield** 260 feet.
7= **Park Plaza Hotel, Leeds** 253 feet.
7= **Tower North Central, Leeds** 253 feet.
9. **Candle house, Leeds** 246 feet.
10. **K2, Leeds** 243 feet.

The Lantern Tower of **York Minster** is 234 feet tall.

SCHOOLS AND COLLEGES

THE BEST STATE SCHOOLS ACCORDING TO A-LEVEL RESULTS IN 2011

1. **Heckmondwike Grammar School**
2. **Ripon Grammar School**
3. **Ermysted's Grammar School**, Skipton
4. **Greenhead College**, Huddersfield
5. **Fulford School**, York
6. **The Crossley Heath School**, Halifax
7. **Skipton Girls' High School**
8. **St Mary's Catholic Comprehensive School**, Menston
9. **Shelley College** - A Specialist Centre for Science
10. **Huntington School**, York

THE BEST SCHOOLS (BOTH INDEPENDENT AND STATE) ACCORDING TO A-LEVEL RESULTS IN 2011

1. **Heckmondwike Grammar School** (20th best school in England)
2. **Ripon Grammar School**
3. **Ermysted's Grammar School**, Skipton
4. **Hymers College**, Kingston-upon-Hull *
5. **Wakefield Girls' High School** *
6. **Greenhead College**
7. **Queen Elizabeth Grammar School**, Wakefield *
8. **Bootham School**, York *
9. **Fulford School**, York
10. **Scarborough College** *
    * Independent school

Schools with the best GCSE results in 2011

Figures are the percentage of pupils gaining five or more GCSEs with grades A*-C. Where schools are tied they are separated by GCSE points which are shown in brackets.

1. **Skipton Girls' High School** 100% (709.1) (5th best school in England)
2. **Heckmondwike Grammar School** 100% (694.4)
3. **The North Halifax Grammar School** 100% (648.3)
4. **Ripon Grammar School** 100% (571.4)
5. **Bradford Girls' Grammar School** 100% (566.4)*
6. **St. Peter's School**, York 100% (539.8)*
7. **Bradford Grammar School** 100% (534.3)*
8. **Birkdale School**, Sheffield 100% (508.1)*
9. **Gateways School**, Harewood 100% (450.5)*
10. **The Crossley Heath School**, Halifax 99% (679.2)

* = independent school

Oldest independent schools

1. **St Peter's School York** 627 AD
   Founded by Saint Paulinus. Alcuin was the headmaster during the 760s. He went on to be Chancellor to the Emperor Charlemagne.
   It's the third oldest school in the country and the fifth oldest school in the world.
   Famous alumni: John Barry, Guy Fawkes.

2. **Hull Collegiate** 1330
   Hull Grammar School was founded in 1330. In 2005 it merged with Hull High School to form Hull Collegiate School.
   Famous alumni: William Wilberforce.

3. **Giggleswick** founded 1512 moved to its present location in 1869.

   Famous alumni: C-3PO (Anthony Daniels) from the Star Wars films, Richard Whiteley. Russell Harty used to teach English and drama.

4. **Pocklington School** founded 1514.
   Famous alumni: Sir Tom Stoppard, Adrian Edmondson.

5. **Bradford Grammar** founded 1548.
   Famous alumni: Frederick Delius, Denis Healey, Sir Ken Morrison, David Hockney, Adrian Moorhouse, Alistair and Jonathan Brownlee.

6. **Leeds Grammar School** 1552 (though there is some evidence that the school existed as early as 1341).

   Famous alumni: Barry Cryer, Sir Gerald Kaufman, Colin Montgomerie, John Smeaton, Ricky Wilson (lead singer of The Kaiser Chiefs).

7. **Queen Elizabeth Grammar School**, Wakefield founded 1591.

   Famous/infamous alumni: Mike Tindall, Edmund Cartwright (inventor of the power loom), John George Haigh (the Acid Bath Murderer), Stephen Griffiths (The Crossbow Cannibal).

8. **Hipperholme Grammar** founded 1648.
   Famous alumni: Sir Robert Peel, Laurence Sterne, Danny and Richard McNamara of Embrace.

9. **The Read School**, Drax, near Selby founded 1667.

10. **Rishworth School** founded 1724.
    Famous alumni: John Noakes.

Batley Grammar School was founded in 1612. It used to be an independent fee-paying school, but has recently become one of the country's first free schools.

Famous alumni: Joseph Priestley, Sir Titus Salt.

Oldest state schools

1. **Beverley Grammar School** was founded in 700 and it's the oldest state school in the world.

   Famous alumni: Thomas Percy (helped to plan The Gunpowder Plot of 1605), Saint John Fischer, Smithson Tennant (chemist who discovered iridium and osmium), Paul Robinson (goalkeeper).

2. **Northallerton College**, formerly Northallerton Grammar School, founded 1323. The Grammar school moved to its present site in 1909.

   Famous alumni Alan Hinkes (mountaineer)

3. **Hall Cross School**, Doncaster, founded 1350. Originally called Doncaster Grammar School

4. **Penistone Grammar School** 1392

5. **Bridlington School**, 1447, originally Bridlington Grammar School

6. **Ermysted's Grammar School**, Skipton, 1492

7. **Bingley Grammar School** 1529
   Famous alumni: Sir Fred Hoyle

8. **Archbishop Holdgate's School**, York, 1546

9. **Ripon Grammar School** 1555
   Famous alumni: William Hague, Richard Hammond, Bruce Oldfield.

10. **Conyer's School** founded in 1590 as the Free Grammar School of Thomas Conyers.

BIGGEST UNIVERSITIES/ COLLEGES OF FURTHER EDUCATION

The numbers are for 2008/9 and include full-time, part-time, undergraduate and postgraduate students.

1. **Sheffield Hallam University** 33,830 (3rd largest university in the UK)
2. **University of Leeds** 33,585 (4th largest)
3. **Leeds Metropolitan University** 27,800
4. **Teesside University** 27,505
5. **University of Sheffield** 24,715
6. **University of Hull** 22,370
7. **University of Huddersfield** 21,590
8. **University of York** 13,490
9. **University of Bradford** 12,740
10. **York St John University** 6,535

HISTORY

A brief history of Yorkshire up to the 12th Century

1. The last Ice Age ended about 10,000 years ago and shortly afterwards stone age hunter-gatherers arrived.

2. About 5,000 years ago stone age farmers began cutting down the forests to make way for farming.

3. The stone age was followed by the bronze age about 4,000 years ago and in about 500 BC the Celts arrived in Yorkshire. Most of what would become North and West Yorkshire was occupied by a tribe called the Brigantes who had their capital at Aldborough. Parts of East Yorkshire were occupied by a tribe called the Parisii.

4. AD 71 the Romans arrived in Yorkshire and built forts in York and Doncaster. Roman towns were created at York, Aldborough (on the site of the old Brigantine capital) and at Brough on Humber.
    By the 4th Century the Roman civilisation was in decline. The last Roman soldiers left Britain in 407 AD. Afterwards the Roman towns were abandoned and the Roman way of life disappeared from Yorkshire.

5. After the Romans had left, small Celtic kingdoms arose in Yorkshire. These eventually became absorbed into the Anglo-Saxon kingdom of Northumbria which eventually stretched from the Irish Sea to the North Sea and from Edinburgh to Hallamshire in South Yorkshire.
    During the Dark Ages most people lived in tiny villages and tilled the soil. In the 8th Century York sprang to life again and became a centre for commerce.

6. Vikings began to raid northern England at the end of the 8th Century. In the mid 9th Century their intentions turned

to conquest and in 866 an army led by Ivar the Boneless invaded Northumbria and captured York. The Vikings named the city Jorvik and made it the capital city of a kingdom bearing the same name. This kingdom of Jorvik covered most of southern Northumbria - an area roughly equivalent to today's Yorkshire. The kingdom of Jorvik was divided into three parts called Threthingr. The Viking kingdom of Jorvik lasted until 954 when it was recaptured by the English.

In 1066 Edward the Confessor, king of England died. Yorkshire became the setting for two major battles that would help decide who would succeed him to the throne. Harold Godwinson was declared King by the English but this was disputed by Harold Hardrada, King of Norway and William Duke of Normandy.

In the late summer of 1066 Harold Hardrada led a large Norwegian fleet and army up the river Humber towards York. Hardrada was met by the army of the northern earls, Edwin of Mercia and Morcar of Northumbria and defeated them at the Battle of Fulford. Harold Hardrada then occupied York and his army encamped at Stamford Bridge. Harold Godwinson had to travel from London gathering his army as he went to face the invaders. On 25th September 1066, Harold Godwinson defeated the Viking army at Stamford Bridge and killed Harold Hardrada. The battle at Stamford Bridge was one of the most pivotal battles in English history. On 28th September William Duke of Normandy landed on the south coast of England. Harold Godwinson rushed south from Yorkshire with his army. They met at the Battle of Hastings where the English army (weakened by the Vikings and the long march) was defeated. Harold Godwinson was killed, allowing William to become King of England.

8. In 1086 the people of Yorkshire rebelled against the Norman conquerors. King William marched to York and built a fort there. However when he left the area in 1069 Yorkshire

rose in rebellion again. This time William took very drastic action. His soldiers destroyed all farming tools, burned all the crops in the fields and slaughtered domestic animals. This 'scorched earth' policy was called the Harrying of the North. As a result of it many people in Yorkshire starved to death. The figure was possibly 100,000.

9. The new Norman rulers built large stone castles at Conisbrough, Tickhill, Pontefract, Richmond, Middleham, Skipsea, York, Scarborough, Pickering and Helmsley.

10. At the end of the 11th Century and the beginning of the 12th, over 60 monasteries were founded in Yorkshire. The first was Selby Abbey, founded in 1069.

A BRIEF HISTORY OF YORKSHIRE FROM THE 13TH CENTURY TO THE 18TH CENTURY

1. Yorkshire eventually recovered from the Harrying of the North and in the 12th and 13th Centuries Yorkshire prospered and many new towns were created. These included Leeds, Hull, Barnsley, Sheffield, Richmond, Scarborough and Northallerton.

2. In the 14th century the climate worsened and in the years 1315-1322 the Great Famine struck.

3. The Black Death arrived in Yorkshire in 1349 and eventually killed about one third of the population.

4. The Wars of the Roses were fought between the Houses of York and Lancaster between 1455 and 1485. The Lancastrians were eventually triumphant and their leader, Henry Tudor, became Henry VII of England.

5. In the 16th century the wool industry became concentrated in Western Yorkshire. The town of Leeds flourished and its population grew rapidly. Wakefield and Halifax also prospered because of the cloth trade.

6. The Pilgrimage of Grace

   Between 1536 and 1540, the dissolution of the monasteries by Henry VIII had a profound and permanent effect on the Yorkshire landscape. Monastic land was divided and sold to form the estates of the gentry and the newly rich industrial entrepreneurs. The unpopularity of Henry VIII's actions resulted in a rising in Lincolnshire which spread to Yorkshire where it became known as the Pilgrimage of Grace.

   In 1536 Robert Aske led a band of 9,000 men, who entered and occupied York. There Aske arranged for the expelled monks and nuns to return to their houses. The king's newly installed tenants were driven out and Catholic observance resumed. The rising was so successful that the royal leaders, the Duke of Norfolk and the Earl of Shrewsbury, were forced to open negotiations with Aske at Scawsby Leys near Doncaster. The king authorised Norfolk to promise a general pardon and a parliament to be held at York within a year, as well as a reprieve for the abbeys until the parliament had met. Aske believed these promises and dismissed his followers. However, within a year Aske and others who had been involved in the Pilgrimage of Grace had been put to death. This enabled the Duke of Norfolk to quell the rising and martial law was imposed upon the demonstrating regions. The dissolution of the monasteries continued unabated.

7. As early as the 14th Century Sheffield was noted for its production of knives. By 1600 Sheffield was the main centre of cutlery production in England.

8. The Battle of Marston Moor near Long Marston in North Yorkshire in 1644 was a decisive battle during the English Civil War. Parliamentarians defeated the Royalists who thereby lost the north of England. This proved a fatal handicap to the Royalists when they tried unsuccessfully to link up with the Scottish Royalists the following year.

   At the end of the civil war many of the castles of Yorkshire such as Helmsley and Pontefract were dismantled so that they could never again be fortified.

9. In the 17th century Scarborough became the country's first seaside holiday resort.

10. In the 18th century the wool industry in Yorkshire flourished. Leeds and the other wool towns continued to grow rapidly.

    The coal mining industry in the West Riding also prospered.

    Industry in Yorkshire was helped by improvements in transport. A number of turnpike roads were built. These were privately owned and you had to pay to use them. In the late 18th century canals were dug.

Yorkshire since the 19th Century

1. In the mid 19th Century York became a centre of the railway industry.

2. Mass unemployment in the 1920s and 1930s.

3. From the 1950s large numbers of West Indian and Asian immigrants came to Yorkshire.

4. In the 1950s the national parks were created: the Peak District (part of which is in Yorkshire) in 1951, North York Moors 1952 and the Yorkshire Dales in 1954.

   The Forest of Bowland was designated an Area of Outstanding Natural Beauty in 1964. At the time much of the area was in the West Riding. Today, a small part is still within North Yorkshire.

   The Howardian Hills were designated an AONB in 1987.

   Nidderdale was designated an AONB in 1994.

   Part of the North Pennines AONB lies within North Yorkshire. It's just 2.6 square kilometres around Tan Hill.

5. In 1974 the political map of Yorkshire changed. It was divided into four local government areas; North Yorkshire, West Yorkshire, South Yorkshire and Humberside.

   Historically, Yorkshire was divided into three ridings and the Ainsty of York. The term 'riding' is of Viking origin and derives from threthingr meaning a third part.

before the 1974 reorganisation

The East and North Ridings of Yorkshire were separated by the River Derwent.

The East Riding extended as far south as the river Humber. The North Riding extended as far north as the river Tees.

The West and North Ridings were separated by the Ouse and the Ure/Nidd watershed.

In 1974 the three ridings of Yorkshire were abolished.

In 1974 the counties of North Yorkshire, West Yorkshire and South Yorkshire were formed. York became part of North Yorkshire. Middlesbrough and Redcar were moved from the North Riding into the newly created county of Cleveland. This new county also included Stockton-on-Tees and Hartlepool, north of the Tees. Much of the East Riding was combined with North Lincolnshire to form the new county of Humberside. This proved very unpopular.

Also in 1974:

Barnoldswick, Slaidburn and the Forest of Bowland were given to Lancashire.
Sedburgh and Dent became part of the new county of Cumbria.
Saddleworth became part of Greater Manchester.
Bowes was given to County Durham.

6. 1 August 1975 - the first Yorkshire Day was celebrated by the Yorkshire Ridings Society as a protest against the local government re-organisation of 1974.

1 of August is also known as Minden Day to certain sections of our armed forces. The Battle of Minden occurred on this date in 1759 and during the battle the King's Own Yorkshire Light Infantry regiment displayed great courage.

1 August is also the anniversary of the emancipation of slaves in the British Empire in 1834. Of course, Yorkshire MP William Wilberforce had campaigned many years for this.

7. The textile and mining industries declined in the 1970s and 1980s.

8. 1986 Fountains Abbey became a UNESCO World Heritage Site. As well as the abbey ruins and Georgian water garden there's also the medieval deer park which is home to about 500 deer.

   2001 Saltaire became a UNESCO World Heritage Site.

9. Hillsborough disaster April 15 1989. 96 Liverpool supporters died and nearly 800 were injured. It remains the deadliest stadium-related disaster in British history. The findings of the Taylor Report resulted in the elimination of standing terraces at all major football stadiums in Britain.

10. In 1996 Cleveland and Humberside were abolished.

    Humberside, north of the river Humber was divided into the East Riding of Yorkshire and the separate unitary authority of Kingston-upon-Hull.

    Cleveland was divided into the separate unitary authorities of Middlesbrough, Hartlepool, Stockton-on-Tees and Redcar and Cleveland. Redcar and Cleveland includes the towns of Redcar, Saltburn-by-the-Sea and Guisborough.

    Middlesbrough and Redcar and Cleveland are once again part of the ceremonial county of North Yorkshire.

Significant historical figures born before 1550

1. **Edwin of Northumbria**
   Born c586, whereabouts unknown. Died 632 or 638 near Doncaster. He was the king of Deira and Bernicia. Deira was a kingdom that extended from the Humber to the Tees and from the North Sea coast to the western edge of the Vale of York. Bernicia covered what is now county Durham, Northumberland and south-eastern Scotland. In the early 7th Century Deira and Bernicia joined to form the kingdom of Northumbria. Edwin became king about 616 and remained king until his death. He converted to Christianity and was baptised in 627. Edwin became the most powerful Anglo-Saxon ruler in Britain but in 632 or 633 he was killed at the Battle of Hatfield Chase near Doncaster. Edwin was defeated by a joint force from Wales and Mercia. The defeat of Edwin and his army resulted in the temporary collapse of the Northumbrian state. What we know about Edwin comes mainly from the writings of the Venerable Bede. After his death, Edwin was venerated as a saint and became known as St. Edwin of Northumbria.

2. **St. Hilda of Whitby**
   614-680. Her actual name was Hild of Streonshal (Streonshal was the old name for Whitby). In 627 she was baptized a Christian in York. In 647 she became a nun and in 657 she founded a monastery at Whitby. The abbey became a centre of both religion and of learning. Hild presided over the Synod of Whitby in 644 which settled the differences between the Roman church and the Celtic church. Detail of Hild's life come from The Ecclesiastical History of the English by the Venerable Bede.

3. **Alcuin of York**
   Born around 735 AD in York and died in 804. He was an ecclesiastic, poet and teacher. He was a scholar and later headmaster at York School (which is now St. Peter's). For a time he was Charlemagne's leading advisor on ecclesiastical and educational matters.

   Buried at St. Martin's Church at Tours in France.

4. **Henry I**
   Born either 1068 or 1069 probably in Selby. He was the fourth son of William the Conqueror. Being the fourth son he was never expected to become king. However, Henry's eldest brother, William II, was killed in a hunting accident in 1100. His second eldest brother, Richard, had died in 1081 and his third eldest brother, Robert, was fighting in the First Crusade. Henry was crowned king of England in 1100 and remained king until his death in 1135. He was buried at Reading Abbey. The Abbey was destroyed during the Reformation and no trace of his grave remains.

5. **Robin Hood**
   Ballads and tales about a character called Robin Hood date from the 15th Century and many place him in the 12th or 13th Centuries. Was he a real person or a fictional character?

   The county of Nottinghamshire has successfully claimed Robin Hood as their own. Indeed, many of the early ballads and accounts mention Sherwood Forest and the Sheriff of Nottingham. However, in medieval times the forest covered a very large area and extended into Derbyshire and Yorkshire.

   There are many connections with the legend in West and South Yorkshire and the earliest ballads suggest that Robin was from the Barnsdale area of what is now in South Yorkshire

   Robin Hood might have died at Kirklees Priory, on the

outskirts of Mirfield, not far from where the Three Nuns pub now sits next to the A62. Part of Kirklees Priory stood on what is now the pub's car park. Nearby is a stone marking the final resting place of Robin.

Legend has it that the Prioress was a relative of Robin's and that she cared for him when he fell ill. On his deathbed, Robin told Little John where to bury him. He shot an arrow from his bedroom window and where the arrow landed was to be his grave site. There is a grave with an inscription on it referring to Robin Hood on private land behind the Three Nuns pub.

6. **John Wycliffe**
Born somewhere between 1320 and 1330 in Ipreswell which is now known as Hipswell near Catterick Garrison. Died 1384. He was a leading theologian and dissident in the Roman Catholic Church. He was dismissed from the University of Oxford in 1381 for his criticism of the Church. Wycliffe had many followers and they were called Lollards and the Lollard movement was a precursor to the Protestant Reformation in the 16th Century. For this reason, Wycliffe is sometimes called the Morning Star of the Reformation. He was the first person to translate the Latin text Bible into English. The Pope was so infuriated by Wycliffe's translation of the Bible and his teachings that 44 years after his death he ordered his bones to be dug up, crushed and scattered in the river.

7. **Richard Plantagenet, also known as Richard of York**
Born 1411 and died 1460. He was the great grandson of Edward III and governed the country as Lord Protector during the madness of Henry VI, who was of the House of Lancaster. Richard's conflicts with Henry's wife, Margaret of Anjou, and other members of Henry's court were a major cause of the Wars of the Roses (1455-1485). Richard had a good claim to the throne of England and it

was agreed by The Act of Accord that he and his heirs would succeed Henry VI. However, Richard was killed at the Battle of Wakefield in 1460 by a Lancastrian force before Henry died. He was buried at Pontefract but his head was put on a pike and displayed over Micklegate Bar in York, wearing a paper crown. His remains were later moved to the Church of St. Mary and All Saints in Fotheringhay, Northamptonshire.

A few months later, Richard's eldest son, Edward, marched on London and was proclaimed King Edward IV in 1461. The House of Lancaster fought to restore Henry VI to the throne, but Edward strengthened his position with a decisive victory at The Battle of Towton at which the Lancastrian army was virtually wiped out.

However, some of Edward's supporters switched to the Lancastrian side and Henry VI was briefly reinstated to the throne in 1470. Edward regained the throne the following year and remained king, without opposition, until his death in 1483. He was succeeded by his 12 year old son, Edward V. He only remained king for two months.

Edward's will appointed his brother Richard as Protector upon his death. Richard placed Edward V and his younger brother in the Tower of London, ostensibly for their own safety. After some political chicanery Richard was made king. The "Princes in the Tower" eventually disappeared, probably murdered by their uncle, now Richard III.

Opposition to Richard's rule led to a revolt aimed at installing Lancastrian Henry Tudor to the throne. In 1485 at the Battle of Bosworth Field Henry Tudor defeated Richard III, bringing an end to The Wars of the Roses. Richard was killed in the battle.

8. **Saint John Fisher**
Born 1469 in Beverley. Died 1535. He was a Roman Catholic bishop and martyr. Fisher was executed by order of Henry VIII during the English Reformation for refusing to

accept him as the supreme head of the Church of England. He was beheaded on Tower Hill. His head was put on a pole on London Bridge, but its ruddy and lifelike appearance caused so much attention that it was thrown into the Thames. His body was buried in the Church of St. Peter ad Vincula by The Tower of London.

He was canonised in 1935. St. John Fisher Catholic high schools in Harrogate and Dewsbury are named after him. St. John's House at Ampleforth College is also named after him.

9. **Mother Shipton**
Born 1488 in Knaresborough. Died 1561. She was born Ursula Southeil, legend has it, in the cave that bears her later name. Although being hideously ugly she married Toby Shipton, a local carpenter in 1512. She told fortunes and made predictions throughout her life. Her prophecies came in the form of poems and allegedly foretold the Great Fire of London in 1666 and the defeat of the Spanish Armada. Mother Shipton's Cave and the nearby petrifying well have been tourist attractions since the 1600s.

10. **William Craven**
Born in Appletreewick in 1548. Died 1618. He went to London at the age of 14 and became apprentice to a cloth merchant. He rapidly worked his way up through the company and eventually took it over and made his fortune. In 1610 he became Lord Mayor of London. Some think that the story of Dick Whittington is based on Craven's life story and he is sometimes called "Aptrick's Dick Whittington". On his return to Appletreewick he enlarged the High Hall, built Burnsall bridge and founded Burnsall Grammar School which is now Burnsall primary school.

Significant historical figures born after 1550

1. **St. Margaret Clitherow**
   Born 1556 in York. Died 1585.

   She is often called the "Pearl of York". She was born Margaret Middleton and married John Clitherow at the age of 15. She bore him three children and at the age of 18 she converted to Roman Catholicism. She regularly held masses at her home in the Shambles. A priest hole was cut in the attic between her house and her neighbour's so that the priest could escape in the event of a raid. She was first imprisoned in 1577 for failing to attend church. She was frequently imprisoned, sometimes for two years at a time.

   An Act of 1581 had outlawed Catholic religious ceremonies and had made sheltering a priest a criminal offence punishable by death. Such a harsh sentence was hardly ever enforced.

   In 1586 she was arrested for harbouring Roman Catholic priests and for holding masses. She refused to plead to the case in order to protect her children. Refusing to plead meant that there would not be a trial at which her children would be forced to testify because they were the only witnesses. The standard punishment for refusing to plead was execution by being crushed to death. She was killed on Good Friday 1586 by the toll-booth on Ouse Bridge. She was stripped and laid on a sharp stone about the size of a man's fist. A door was put on top of her and slowly loaded with stones until the sharp stone broke her back. It took an agonising 15 minutes for her to die. After her death her right hand was removed and it's now housed in the chapel of the Bar Convent in York. The resting place of her body is not known. Elizabeth I wrote to the people of York to say how horrified she was at the treatment of Margaret; because of her gender she should not have been executed.

Margaret Clitherow was beatified in 1929 and canonised in 1970. A number of schools in England are named after her. The Shrine of Margaret Clitherow is located in a house on the Shambles.

2. Guy Fawkes

Britain's most notorious traitor. Born 1570 in Stonegate, York. Hung, drawn and quartered in 1606 in Old Palace Yard at Westminster, opposite the building he had tried to blow up.

In 1604 Fawkes became involved with a small group of English Catholics, led by Robert Catesby, who planned to assassinate the Protestant King James I. They planned to blow up the House of Lords on the opening of Parliament. 36 barrels of gunpowder were hidden in the cellars beneath the House of Lords and it was Fawkes' job to light the fuse.

Some of Fawkes' co-conspirators were worried that a number of Catholics would be present in the House of Lords. As a result one of them sent an anonymous letter to Lord Monteagle warning him to stay away from Parliament on the 5th of November. The letter was shown to the King and the cellars were searched and Fawkes and the gunpowder discovered.

As was tradition, after being hung, drawn and quartered, his remains were sent to the four corners of the kingdom.

3. Thomas Fairfax

Born 1612 at Denton Hall near Otley. Died 1671. He was a leading parliamentary general during the English Civil War (1642-51). He played a very important part in the defeat of Royalist forces at the Battle of Marston Moor in 1644. In 1645 parliament decided to form a new professional army and Fairfax was made commander-in-chief. Fairfax moulded this New Model Army into a disciplined fighting force and in June 1645 the army inflicted a serious defeat upon the Royalists at Naseby. This effectively ended any chance Charles I had of winning the war.

At the end of the civil war Fairfax opposed the execution of king Charles I. In 1660 Fairfax supported General Monck's successful attempt to restore the monarchy.

4. Thomas Chippendale

Born in Farnley near Otley in 1718. Died 1778. Buried at St. Martin-in-the-Field Church in London. Perhaps the most famous furniture maker ever. Chippendale lived and worked in London but he did take on several large scale commissions in Yorkshire. These include Temple Newsam, Nostell Priory, Newby Hall, Harewood House and Burton Constable Hall.

5. Captain James Cook

Born 1728 in the village of Marton, which is now part of Middlesbrough. He died in 1779 in Hawaii. He was the greatest explorer of the 18th Century. His achievements are all the more remarkable considering his humble beginnings from an agricultural labouring family.

On his first voyage to the Pacific in the *Endeavour* (1768-71) Lieutenant Cook (as he was called at that time) charted over 5,000 of previously unknown coastline around New Zealand and eastern Australia.

On his second voyage (1772-75), this time in the *Resolution*, the newly promoted Captain Cook carried one of John Harrison's famous no. 4 marine chronometer which allowed an accurate reading of time and longitude to be made at sea. This instrument allowed Cook to produce the first accurate maps of the lands of the south Pacific.

On his third and final voyage (1776-80), again in the *Resolution*, he turned his attention to the north Pacific. He discovered the Hawaiian Islands and put the main outline of the coast of north-west America on the map.

On his return to the Hawaiian islands in 1790 he was killed during a fight with natives. They took his body, disembowelled it and removed the flesh so that the bones could be preserved. Some of his remains were returned to be buried at sea.

The Captain Cook monument stands on Easby Moor overlooking the village of Great Ayton, which was the childhood home of Cook.

6. William Wilberforce

Born 1759 in Kingston-upon-Hull. Died 1833.

Wilberforce was a deeply religious member of Parliament and social reformer. He led the parliamentary campaign against the slave trade for nearly 30 years until it was abolished by the Slave Trade Act of 1807. However, slavery still continued, as it was only the trading of slaves that was abolished. Wilberforce continued his campaign until the Slavery Abolition Act of 1833, which ended slavery in most of the British Empire. Wilberforce died three days after hearing of the passing of the Act. He was buried in Westminster Abbey.

7. Mary Bateman - The Yorkshire Witch

Born in Asenby near Thirsk in 1768. Died 1809. She was commonly called the Yorkshire Witch and was executed for murder by poisoning. At the end of the 18th Century she became a fortune teller in Leeds. She prescribed potions which she claimed would ward off evil spirits as well as acting as medicine. Some of her potions contained poison. Bateman was hanged in York for fraud and murder in 1809. After her execution her body was put on public and strips of her skin were sold as magic charms to ward off evil spirits. Her skeleton can be seen in the Thackray Museum in Leeds.

8. **Richard Oastler**

Born in Leeds in 1789. Died 1861.

Oastler was a supporter of the rigid class structure but he believed that it was the responsibility of the ruling class to protect the weak and vulnerable. He campaigned for better working conditions for children - in fact a maximum working day of ten hours. At the time many children worked up to 16 hours per day, often in horrible conditions.

Oastler achieved some success when the 1847 Factory Act restricted children to a ten hour day in cotton mills. In 1867 the Act was widened to encompass children working in all factories. There's a statue of Oastler in Northgate, Bradford and a school in Armley is named after him.

9. **Thomas Crapper**

Born in Thorne near Doncaster in 1836. Died 1910. Contrary to widespread misconceptions, Crapper did not invent the flush toilet. However, he did much to increase the popularity of the toilet and he did invent the floating ballcock. Crapper worked as a plumber in London and in 1861 set himself up as a sanitary engineer with his own brass foundry and workshops. He was noted for the quality of his products and received several royal warrants to install plumbing and toilets in royal residencies.

10. **Reverand Benjamin Waugh**

Born 1839 in Settle. Died 1908. Waugh worked as a Congregational minister in the slums of Greenwich. He became appalled by the deprivations and cruelties suffered by children. In 1889 he founded the National Society for the Prevention of Cruelty to Children. Waugh was its first director and Queen Victoria its first patron.

Battlefields

Yorkshire contains more important battlefields than any other county in the UK.

1. **Battle of Fulford Gate** 1066
    This battle took place on 20 September, five days before the Battle of Stamford Bridge. It was fought between the forces of Viking king Hardrada and the northern earls, Morcar of Northumbria and his brother Edwin of Mercia. There were extremely heavy casualties on both sides, with the Vikings being victorious.

2. **Battle of Stamford Bridge** 1066
    When Edward the Confessor died with no direct heir, the throne passed to Harold of Wessex. However, there were two other claimants to the throne. They were William of Normandy and the Viking king Harald Hardrada. The latter landed with an army in Yorkshire. Harold ended the Viking threat at Stamford Bridge on 25 September. Although the battle was a great triumph for Harold, it seriously weakened his forces and shortly afterwards he faced an even greater foe at the Battle of Hastings.
    There is a small stone monument to the battle in the village of Stamford Bridge, which is approximately seven miles east of York.

3. **Battle of the Standard** at Northallerton 22 August 1138, English forces repelled a Scottish army on Cowton Moor. The invaders were led by King David I of Scotland and the English were commanded by William of Aumale. David had entered England to increase his territories and also to support his niece Matilda's claim to the English throne. Much of Northumberland had already fallen to the Scots, but heavy losses and defeat at Northallerton caused them to fall back to Carlisle.

4. **Myton Meadows** 20 September 1319
Despite the famous Scottish victory at Bannockburn in 1314, war between Scotland and England continued. A Scottish army led by the Earl of Moray marched on York. A force, of mainly Yorkshire militia, met them at Myton, which is three miles east of Boroughbridge. Myton was an easy victory for the Scots and perhaps 4,000 English out of a total force of 20,000 were killed. The battle resulted in the end to the English siege of Berwick. This had been the Scot's aim as after Myton, they retreated back to their homeland.

5. **Boroughbridge** 1322
Thomas, Earl of Lancaster, who was in collusion with the Scots, was defeated by Sir Andrew Harcla, Edward II's general.

6. **Battle of Bramham Moor** 1408
At the battle the Percys tried to overthrow King Henry. There is a memorial stone to the battle on the A1 access road called Paradise Way between Bramham Village and Bramham crossroads.

7. **Battle of Wakefield** 30 December 1460
This was a major battle of the Wars of the Roses and took place at Sandal near Wakefield. Richard of York was killed and his army destroyed. The battle maybe the source for the mnemonic for remembering the colours of the rainbow: Richard of York gave battle in vain.

8. **Battle of Towton** 1461 (South of Tadcaster)
It was the largest and bloodiest battle ever fought on English soil.
    The battle took place during the Wars of the Roses in 1461 on 29 March (Palm Sunday) during a snow storm. The House of York won the battle and as a result Edward

IV was crowned king of England. 50,000 soldiers fought each other and 28,000 died. A re-enactment of the battle takes place on Palm Sunday of each year.

9. **Battle of Adwalton Moor** 30 June 1643
   After Marston Moor, this was the second most important action fought in the north during the English Civil War. The Royalist army, led by the Earl of Newcastle, defeated the Parliamentarians led by Lord Fairfax. The battle consolidated Royalist control of Yorkshire. Adwalton is now part of the village of Drighlington, which is between Leeds and Bradford.

10. **Battle of Marston Moor** 1644 (near Tockwith village)
    One of the most important battles during the English Civil War. Oliver Cromwell led an army of Roundheads (Parliamentarians) to victory over the Royalists led by Prince Rupert.

Disasters in Yorkshire

In this list I haven't included battles or events such as the Harrying of the North and episodes of the plague. I've also put mining disasters in a separate list.

1. **Great Sheffield Flood** 1864
   On 11 March 1864 the Dale Dyke Dam at Low Bradfield broke while it was being flooded for the first time. The resulting flood swept down the Loxley valley, into Sheffield city centre, past the sites of today's Don Valley Stadium and Meadowhall and on to Rotherham. 270 people were killed.

2. **Clifford's Tower**, York 1190
   At the site of Clifford's Tower, the keep of York's medieval castle, 150 Jews died in what is the most appalling example of antisemitism in medieval England. On the night of 16 March 1190, the feast of Shabbat ha-Gadol, the small Jewish community of York had assembled together inside the tower for protection. Rather than die at the hands of the angry mob outside, many of the Jews took their own lives and others died in the flames that they had lit. This horrendous event was the culmination of a tide of violent feeling that had swept the country that year. The stone tower that you see today dates back to the 13th Century.

3. **Hillsborough Disaster** 1989
   On 15 April 1989 Liverpool and Nottingham Forest were to play an F.A. Cup semi-final at the home of Sheffield Wednesday. A crush occurred which killed 96 people, all of them Liverpool fans. It is the worst stadium disaster in British history.

4. **HMHS Rohilla** ran aground off Whitby 30 October 1914. 85 killed.

Rohilla was a steamship of the British India Steam Navigation Company. At the outset of World War 1 it was converted into a naval hospital ship. Whilst sailing south down the North Sea, HMHS *Rohilla* struck a rock off the coast of Whitby. The accident happened during a storm and so although the ship was only 600m from shore 85 of the 229 people on board were lost.

5. **Holmfirth flood** 1852
On 5 February 1852 the embankment of the Bilberry reservoir collapsed, flooding the Holme valley. 81 died.

6. **Great Gale** of 1871, Bridlington.
This occurred on 10 February 1871. There were an estimated 70 fatalities at sea, including the crew of Royal National Lifeboat, *Harbinger*.

7. **Masbrough Boat Disaster**
It's also known as the Rotherham Boat Disaster. It happened at a boat yard on the river Don in Masbrough on 5 July 1841. The disaster took place at the launching of the sea-going riverboat the *John and William*. Local teachers and children had been invited to the launch and were gathered on the ship's deck. The narrowness of the river meant that ships were launched sideways. To see the rush of water, everyone ran to the side of the ship as it was launched. It's thought that this is what caused it to capsize. 64 people, mainly children, drowned.

8. **Bradford City Stadium Fire** 1985
On 11 May 1985 Bradford City were playing Lincoln City. The day was supposed to be a celebration of Bradford winning the third division title. A flash fire swept through one side of the Valley Parade Stadium and 56 people died.

9. **Booth's clothing factory fire**, Huddersfield, 31 October 1941. 49 killed. The blaze, which began just after 8am, was caused by a worker putting a smouldering pipe into a jacket pocket. Workers on the upper floors were trapped. There were no emergency exits. Of the 150 workers that had been in the building, 49 perished.

10. **ZR-2 airship** crashed into the Humber estuary, 24 August 1921. 44 out of the 49 crew were killed.

    The R-38 class of airship was designed for use by the Royal Navy towards the end of World War 1. They were intended for long-range patrol duties over the North Sea. Four of these airships had been ordered by the admiralty, but the 1918 armistice led to the cancellation of this order. However, the United States Navy agreed to purchase one of them. At the time of her launch in 1921, the R-38, was the largest airship in the world. On 24 August 1921, the newly designated ZR-2 was destroyed by a structural failure whilst flying over Hull and crashed into the Humber estuary. 44 of the 49 crew were killed. This was more deaths than occurred in the more famous Hindenburg disaster of 1937. 35 died in that.

Mining disasters

1. **Oaks Colliery**, near Stairfoot, Barnsley. 12 December 1866. 361 miners and rescuers were killed. The disaster was caused by the explosions of flammable gases. It remains the worst colliery disaster in England and the second worst in the UK.

2. **Lundhill Colliery**, Barnsley, 19 February 1857. 189 died.

3. **Swaithe Main**, Worsbrough near Barnsley, 6 December 1875. 143 killed.

4. **Combs Pit**, Thornhill, Dewsbury, 4 July 1893. 139 killed.

5. **Cadeby Main Colliery**, Doncaster, 9 July 1912. 88 killed.

6. **Darley Main**, Barnsley, 24 January 1849. 75 killed.

7. **Ardsley Main**, Barnsley, 5 March 1847. 73 killed.

8. **Oaks Colliery**, Barnsley, 24 January 1847. 70 killed.

9. **Micklefield Colliery** near Leeds, 30 April 1896. 62 killed.

10. **Edmunds Main**, Worsbrough near Barnsley, 8 December 1862. 59 killed.

WORST MINING DISASTERS SINCE 1900

1. **Cadeby Main Colliery**, Doncaster, 9 July 1912. 88 killed.

2. **Wharncliffe Woodmoor Colliery** near Barnsley. 6 August 1936. 58 killed.

3. **Bentley Colliery** near Doncaster. 20 November 1931. 45 killed.

4. **Maltby Main Colliery** near Rotherham. 28 July 1923. 27 killed.

5. **Crigglestone Colliery** near Wakefield. 29 July 1941. 22 killed.

6. **North Gawber** (Lidgett) 12 September 1935. 19 killed.

7. **Barnsley Main Colliery** 16 February 1942. 13 killed.

8. **Ingham Colliery**, Thornhill, Dewsbury. 9 September 1947. 12 killed.

9. **Wharncliffe Colliery**, Silkstone. 30 May 1914. 11 killed.

10. **South Kirkby Colliery**, Wakefield. 23 August 1935. 10 killed.

Important events in the history of York up to 1100

1. York was founded in AD71 when the Roman General
    Quintus Petillius Cerialis and the Ninth Legion constructed
    a military fortress on flat ground where the river Foss
    meets the river Ouse. A large and important town grew up
    around the fortress and this settlement was called Eburaci
    or Eboracum.

2. During his stay in the early part of the 3rd Century,
    Emperor Septimius Severus proclaimed Eboracum the
    capital of Britannia Inferior. Londinium was the capital of
    Britannia Superior. Severus died in Eboracum in 211.
    About this time stone walls were built around the fortress
    to replace the original wooden ones. The Multangular
    Tower and the lengths of wall to either side of it are the
    only sections of the wall that remain.

3. In 306 Constantius I died during his stay in York and his
    son, Constantine, was proclaimed Emperor by the troops
    in the fortress. He went on to become Constantine the
    Great. He founded Constantinople and was the first
    Roman emperor to convert to Christianity. There is a statue
    of him outside York Minster.

4. During the early 400s the Romans left York and Britain.

5. 627 a wooden minster was built for the Saxon king Edwin
    of Northumbria. He had converted to Christianity and he
    chose York for his baptism.
    In the 700s Eboracum became known as Eoforwic and
    was the capital of the kingdom of Northumbria.

6. 866 Vikings under Ivar the Boneless capture Eoforwic.
    Between 866 and 954 the city, now called Jorvik was

effectively the capital of the new Viking kingdom called the Danelaw.

7. 954 The last Viking king, Eric the Bloodaxe, was defeated and killed. From then on York and Northumbria were always part of a united Anglo-Saxon kingdom.

8. 1066 The Battles of Fulford and Stamford Bridge near York (as it was now known) severely weakened King Harold's army before its defeat against William the Conqueror at Hastings.

9. 1068 William I marched into York. In 1069 William built two castles in York - they were sited on either side of the Ouse, one on Clifford's Tower and the other on Baille Hill. A chain could be stretched between them to prevent passage along the river. Local rebellions against William resulted in the Harrying of the North.

10. 1080-1100 the first stone Norman minster is built. In 1070 Thomas of Bayeux had been appointed the first Norman Archbishop of York.

IMPORTANT EVENTS IN THE HISTORY OF YORK FROM 1100

1. **1190** Massacre of 150 Jews in Clifford's Tower

2. **1220** Building of the present Minster begins.

3. **1240** to **1340** the present city walls are built. The walls are two and a half miles long. The walls today still retain all four

of their impressive gateways into the city called bars. The paved walkway on the inside of the walls was built by the Victorians. The wall seems to disappear midway between Monk Bar and Walmgate Bar. However, there never was a wall here because in medieval times this part of York was marshland and so a wall here wasn't necessary.

4. **1298** Because of his wars with Scotland, Edward I moved the Chancery and the Exchequer to York. They only returned to London in 1304. For those years, York was effectively the capital of England. The city was also used as the base for Edward's army.

5. **1328** sees a royal wedding. Edward III married Philippa of Hainault at York Minster. She was 13 and he was 15. Edward had become king a few months earlier.

6. **1385** Richard II created the title Duke of York, first bestowed on his uncle, Edmund of Langley. Since the late 15th Century the title, when granted, has usually been given to the second son of the British monarch. Prince Andrew is the 14th Duke of York.

7. **1472** York Minster is completed and consecrated.

8. **1739** Highwayman Dick Turpin is hanged at Tyburn.

9. **1871-77** Present railway station built. At the time it was the largest railway station in the world. As part of the new station development the Royal Station Hotel (now The Royal York Hotel) was opened in 1878.

10. **1984** Fire at York Minster. Probably started by lightning, it destroyed the roof of the south transept as well as the famous rose window.

IMPORTANT EVENTS IN THE HISTORY OF BRADFORD UP TO 1850

1. Bradford began as a village by a ford. Brad means broad. At the time of the Doomsday Book in 1086 the village by the broad ford had a population of about 300.

2. Medieval Bradford had a population of several hundred and had three streets. They were Kirkgate, Westgate and Ivegate. The word gate is derived from the old Danish word "gata" meaning street.

3. During the Middle Ages there was a leather tanning industry in Bradford. A wool industry also developed. Wool was woven in the town.

4. Plague struck Bradford in 1557-8. There was another outbreak of plague in 1645.

5. During the English Civil War in the 1640s the townspeople of Wakefield sided with Parliament. The surrounding countryside sided with King Charles.

6. In the late 17th Century people in Bradford began to make worsted instead of woollen cloth.

7. In the early 18th Century Bradford was a small market town with a population of about 4,000.

8. In the late 18th Century the industrial revolution transformed Bradford. Bradford canal was built in 1774 and in 1777 it was connected to the Leeds-Liverpool canal. In 1793 a Piece Hall was built where cloth could be bought and sold.

9. During the 19th Century Bradford became the worsted capital of the world. It's population rose from about 6,000 in 1800 to 103,000 in 1850. Conditions in the "dark Satanic mills" were terrible. Housing was worse. There were no sewers or drains and overcrowding was common. Some families lived in cellars and had no furniture. In 1848-9 a cholera epidemic killed 460.

10. The railway reached Bradford in 1846.

IMPORTANT EVENTS IN THE HISTORY OF BRADFORD SINCE 1850

1. **Titus Salt** built Saltaire between 1853 and 1871. The village had good quality houses, schools, a bath house, a hospital, a library and a church.

2. **Peel Park** (Bradford's first park) opened in 1863.

3. **City Hall** was built in 1873.

4. **Bradford** was made a city in 1897.

5. **The Alhambra Theatre** opened in 1914.

6. In 1919 the Church of St. Peter became Bradford Cathedral.

7. In the 1920s and 30s the textile industry in Bradford declined rapidly and mass unemployment resulted.

8. In the 1950s Bradford became a multi-cultural city with large-scale immigration from the West Indies and the Indian sub-continent.

9. **Bradford University** opened in 1966.

10. In 1985 a fire at Bradford City's football stadium, Valley Parade, killed 56.

IMPORTANT EVENTS IN THE HISTORY OF LEEDS

The name Leeds is derived from Loidis which was the name given to the forest which covered most of the kingdom of Elmet. Very little is known about the settlement's history in Roman and medieval times.

1. **1086** the settlement is referred to as Ledes in the Doomsday Book. According to the book Ledes was a purely agricultural area about 1,000 acres in size with a population of about 200. There was a priest, a church and a mill which was worth four shillings. Ledes was part of lands owned by Ilbert de Lacy, who was one of the favourites of William I. De Lacy's main stronghold was Pontefract castle.

2. **1147** Cistercian monks settled at Kirkstall and from about 1152 began to build Kirkstall Abbey. The monks were great sheep farmers and they had a great deal to do with Leeds eventually developing as a woollen centre. The abbey owned about 5,000 sheep.

3. **1643** In the early part of the English Civil War the town was garrisoned by Sir William Saville who led a Royalist force. Leeds was still a small town. Sir Thomas Fairfax, leading a Parliamentarian army marched on Leeds and easily defeated Saville.

4. **1715** The first history of Leeds was written by Ralph Thoresby. He described Leeds as mainly a merchant town, manufacturing woollen cloths and trading with Europe via the Humber estuary. The size and prosperity of Leeds grew greatly in the 1700s. By the 1770s Leeds was responsible for 30% of the country's woollen exports.

5. **1720** Daniel Defoe visited Leeds and described the town's cloth market as "a prodigy of its kind and not to be equalled in the world".

6. **1758** The Middleton Railway was founded. It carried coal from the Middleton pits into the centre of Leeds. At first it was horse-drawn. In 1812 the Middleton Steam Railway became the first to use steam locomotives.

7. **1816** The Leeds to Liverpool Canal was completed. This made the shipment of textiles to America much easier.

8. **1834** The Leeds and Selby Railway opened. It was the first mainline railway in Yorkshire.

9. **1861** The Corn Exchange was built.

10. **1893** Leeds was granted city status.

IMPORTANT EVENTS IN THE HISTORY OF SHEFFIELD

Sheffield gets its name from the river Sheaf and from the Old English word feld which meant open land without trees.

1. **12th Century**. Sheffield was founded in the 1100s when William de Lovetot built a motte and bailey castle on the site of Castle Market. He also built a church on the site of Sheffield Cathedral. A village grew up between the castle and the church. This was often the way in medieval England. The garrison at the castle provided a market for the townspeople's goods and the castle provided protection for the townspeople and nearby farmers.

2. **1266** A group of barons who supported Simon de Montfort's rebellion against Henry III, marching from north Lincolnshire to Derbyshire, passed through Sheffield and destroyed the town, burning the church and castle.

3. **1270** Thomas de Furnival was given permission by Henry III to rebuild the castle in stone.

4. **1296** A charter to hold a weekly market and an annual fair in Sheffield was granted by Edward I to Thomas de Furnival, Lord of the Manor of Sheffield.

5. **1624** The Company of Cutlers in Hallamshire was established by a Parliamentary Act. Its aim for the past 400 years has been to maintain the standards and quality of Sheffield made cutlery and steel products.

6. **1648** Sheffield Castle was destroyed during the English Civil War.

7. **1770** Benjamin Huntsman, who had invented a method for making better quality steel called crucible steel or cast steel, set up production in Attercliffe, which later became the main location for the Sheffield steel industry.

8. **Thomas Boulsover** discovered a way of plating copper with silver. This silver plate, which came to be known as Sheffield plate, was much cheaper than solid silver and was used for making things like candlesticks and snuff boxes.

9. **1893** Sheffield was made a city.

10. **1913** The first stainless steel was cast in Sheffield.

IMPORTANT EVENTS IN THE HISTORY OF SCARBOROUGH

1. **966** Thorgil nicknamed Skarthi (meaning hare-lip) and his Vikings decided to settle in the place they called Skarthi's Burgh (burgh meant fort or fortified settlement).

2. **1136** Scarborough Castle was built by William Le Gros, Earl of Albermarle. In 1157 Henry II took over the castle and strengthened it by building a new keep. Soon, a little town grew up around the castle.

3. **1253** King Henry III granted a charter for the first Scarborough Fair. During the late middle ages the town was a busy market town and port. The fair was a huge six week trading event, starting 15th August. Merchants came to it from all areas of England, Europe, the Baltic and the Byzantine Empire.

The traditional Scarborough Fair lasted for five centuries but no longer exists, however, a number of celebrations take place every September to mark the original event.

4. **1626** Mrs Elizabeth Farrow discovered a spring at the bottom of the cliffs containing iron. Soon people came from all over Yorkshire to drink from the spa water, which they believed could cure all sorts of ailments. Dr Wittie published a book in 1660 about the spa waters and this attracted many visitors to the town. Scarborough Spa became Britain's first seaside resort.

5. **1732** George II passed an Act to enlarge the harbour by building Vincent's Pier and the present East Pier at a cost of £12,000. At the time there were over 300 sailing ships belonging to Scarborough. Vincent's Pier was completed in 1752. It was named after its engineer William Vincent.

   In the 1750s work began on the construction of the East Pier. John Smeaton, who built the Eddystone Lighthouse, was the consulting engineer. It took over half a century before the pier, measuring 1380 feet, was finally completed.

   The West Pier was built during the early 19th Century.

6. **1735** The first rolling bathing machines were used on the beaches.

7. **1738** Spa destroyed by an earthquake.

8. **1845** Scarborough-Malton-York Railway opened. In 1867 The Grand Hotel was completed and it was one of the largest hotels in the world. Four towers represent the seasons, 12 floors represent the months, 52 chimneys represent the weeks and originally 365 bedrooms represented the days of the year.

9. **1914** Town bombarded by two German warships. 19 people are killed and the lighthouse was destroyed. There was also damage to the Royal Hotel, Grand Hotel and the Town Hall. The furthest bomb damage was three miles inland on a farm.

10. **1993** Landslides at the Holbeck Hill pull the Holbeck Hill Hotel into the sea.

IMPORTANT EVENTS IN THE HISTORY OF WHITBY

1. **657** The building of the first abbey marked the birth of the town. It was founded by Oswy, King of Northumberland. Oswiu's granddaughter Hilda, formerly of Hartlepool Abbey, was made its abbess. Hilda had many devout followers and had a reputation of being holy, wise and kind. After her death she was venerated as a saint. It's thought that Hilda first recognised and encouraged the talents of Caedmon. The monastery was destroyed by Vikings in 867. In 657 Whitby was known as Streonshal.

2. **664** The Synod of Whitby. King Oswiu ruled that his kingdom would calculate Easter and observe the monastic tonsure according to the customs of Rome, rather than the customs practiced by Iona (Celtic) and its satellite institutions.

   Christianity in Britain at the time existed in two forms following Ionan and Roman traditions. The Ionan practice was that of the Irish monks who resided in a monastery on the isle of Iona, whereas the Roman practice followed the customs of Rome.

   In the kingdom of Northumbria (remember that Yorkshire

didn't exist yet), the two traditions coexisted. The Synod of Whitby established Roman practice as the norm in Northumbria. The episcopal seat of Northumbria was transferred from Lindisfarne to York.

3. **1078** Whitby Abbey was refounded. In 2010, Whitby Abbey was voted the most romantic ruins in Britain.

4. **1747** James Cook moved to Whitby at the age of 18 to work for the Walker family who were Quaker ship owners engaged in the transport of coal between Whitby and London. A few years later Cook commanded *HMS Endeavour* on a scientific expedition to the Pacific. *Endeavour* was a Whitby-built collier, solid and flat-bottomed and thus easy to beach and repair. Whitby has a long tradition of ship building. In 1790–91 the town built 11,754 tons of shipping, making it the third largest shipbuilder in England, after London and Newcastle.

5. **1753** The Whitby Whaling Company was established and set off from Whitby harbour to Greenland with two ships. Between 1753 and 1833 there were 55 whaling ships operating from the harbour. The most successful year was 1814 when eight ships caught 172 whales. Whitby's whaling industry came to an end in 1837 after a succession of unsuccessful trips and the final ship returned empty.

It is thought that Whitby's whaling industry was responsible for the harvest of over 25,000 seals, 55 polar bears and 2,761 whales. Boiler houses were built alongside the harbour to render blubber into oil. If the fleet returned home after a successful trip, whale jaw bones were attached to the ship's mast to show that the ship was full. This tradition is marked by Whitby's monumental whale jaw archway. The original bones were given to the town by Norwegian Thor Dhal and the artist Graham

Leach in 1963 in recognition of the dangers faced by the whalers and as a tribute to Whitby's famous whaling history. Those bones decayed and were replaced in 2002. The current whale bones where donated by Whitby's sister town of Anchorage in Alaska.

6. **1808** Whitby's first jet shop opened. Jet became very popular during the Victorian era. Jet, owing to its dark and sombre colour has often been associated with mourning and Queen Victoria wore Whitby jet jewellery as part of her mourning dress after Prince Albert died in 1861.

   Jet is a black or dark brown stone derived from decaying monkey puzzle trees. During the mid Jurassic period trees were washed into the sea and combined with mud and other deposits to form a sedimentary layer on the sea bed. The huge amount of pressure caused by the building up of this sedimentary layer cause the wood to slowly turn to jet.

7. **1839** The railway arrived. The railway connected Whitby to Pickering and eventually to York. George Hudson was responsible for the development of the Royal Crescent. George Stephenson was engineer to the Whitby and Pickering Railway.

8. **1890** Bram Stoker wrote his novel *Dracula* whilst staying in Whitby.

9. **1914** On 30 October the hospital ship *Rohilla* sank after hitting the rocks at Saltwick Bay. Of the 229 people on board, 85 lost their lives. Most are buried in the churchyard at Whitby.

10. **2006** The town was awarded "Best Seaside Resort" by *Which? Holiday* magazine.

TOURISM,
PLACES OF
INTEREST,
LANDSCAPE
AND
LEISURE

This is God's own county. The biggest and most beautiful county in England. Two and a bit national parks. Two areas of outstanding natural beauty. Two World Heritage Sites. Why do people yearn to travel far and wide when they haven't even seen what's on their own doorstep? Yorkshire is a place full of beauty and excitement.

The big cities and towns like Leeds, Sheffield, York, Harrogate and Skipton are great places for a romantic weekend break or even a longer holiday. Villages such as Helmsley and Hawes are also brilliant places to stay.

PLACES TO VISIT IN OR NEAR HELMSLEY

1. **Castle Howard**
2. **North York Moors Steam Railway**
3. **Rievaulx Abbey**
4. **Sutton Bank**
5. **Ampleforth College**
6. **Helmsley Castle**
7. **James Herriot Museum, Thirsk**
8. **Duncombe Park**
9. **Newburgh Priory**
10. **Byland Abbey**

Places to visit in or near Hawes

1. **Aysgarth Falls**
2. **Bolton Castle**
3. **Wensleydale Creamery**
4. **Hardraw Force**
5. **Middleham Castle**
6. **Wensleydale Railway**
7. **Tan Hill Inn** (the drive there from Hawes is superb and takes in the Buttertubs Pass)
8. **White Scar Cave** near Ingleton
9. **Snaizeholme red squirrel trail**
10. **Forbidden Corner**

Places to visit in or near Ripon

1. **Fountains Abbey**
2. **How Stean Gorge**
3. **Brimham Rocks**
4. **Newby Hall**
5. **Ripley Castle**
6. **Himalayan Gardens** at Grewelthorpe (have a look at Hackfall woods while you're there)
7. **Ripon Cathedral**
8. **Thorp Perrow Arboretum**
9. **Black Sheep Brewery** at Masham
10. **Jervaulx Abbey** (you must also stop at the Brymor ice cream parlour)

Harrogate is situated midway between Ripon and Leeds, so most of the places mentioned above and below are close by, especially Harewood House and Ripley Castle. In Harrogate there's also RHS Harlow Carr Gardens.

Places to visit in or near York

1. **York Minster**
2. **National Railway Museum**
3. **Castle Museum and Clifford's Tower**
4. **Medieval city walls**
5. **Yorkshire Museum, Gardens and St Mary's Abbey**
6. **Eden Camp** near Malton
7. **Beningbrough Hall and Gardens**
8. **Royal Air Force Museum**, Elvington
9. **Murton Park** which is home to the Yorkshire Museum of Farming, Danelaw Dark Age Village, Brigantium Roman Fort, the Tudor Croft and the Home Front Experience.
10. **York Dungeon**

Places to visit in or near Leeds

1. **Harewood House**
2. **Temple Newsham**
3. **Nostell Priory**, Wakefield
4. **Royal Armouries Museum**
5. **Kirkstall Abbey and Abbey House Museum**
6. **City Art Gallery** - contains works by Constable, Turner, Henry Moore
7. **Thackray Museum** - Telling the story of medicine
8. **National Coal Mining Museum**, Wakefield
9. **Yorkshire Sculpture Park**
10. **Hepworth Gallery**, Wakefield

Places to visit in or near Sheffield

Some of these are across the border in Derbyshire but that doesn't matter. If you enjoy visiting historic houses then Sheffield must be the best city in the country to stay.

1. **Chatsworth House**
2. **Castleton show caves**
3. **Bolsover Castle**
4. **Renishaw Hall and Gardens**
5. **Haddon Hall**
6. **Brodsworth Hall and Gardens**
7. **Yorkshire Wildlife Park**
8. **Tropical Butterfly House, Wildlife and Falconry Centre**
9. **Wentworth Castle Gardens**
10. **Sheffield Botanical Gardens**

Places to visit in or near Skipton

1. **Haworth for the Bronte Parsonage Museum**
2. **Bolton Abbey** - picturesque abbey beside the river Wharfe
3. **Settle to Carlisle railway**. The most scenic line in England. You can catch the train at Skipton.
4. **Ingleton waterfalls walk**
5. **Saltaire**
6. **Malham Cove and Gordale Scar**
7. **Stump Cross Caverns** near Grassington
8. **Ingleborough Cave**
9. **Parcevall Hall Gardens** near Burnsall
10. **White Scar Caves**

Hotels in Yorkshire

This list is based on AA ratings and my experience.

1= **De Vere Oulton Hall**, Leeds, AA five star.
1= **Cedar Court Grand Hotel and Spa**, York, AA five star.
3= **Crathorne Hall**, Yarm, AA four red stars.
3= **The Devonshire Arms Country House** hotel and spa AA four red stars.
3= **Middlethorpe Hall and Spa Hotel**, York AA four red stars.
3= **Rudding Park Hotel** AA four red stars.
Awarded the title of "Number One Hotel in the UK" in the TripAdvisor Travellers' Choice Awards which honour the world's finest hotels. It was voted sixth best hotel in the world.
3= **Swinton Park Hotel**, Masham, AA four red stars.
3= **Wood Hall Hotel**, Wetherby, AA four red stars.
3= **The Feversham Arms and Verbena Spa hotel**, Helmsley, AA four red stars.
AA Hotel of the Year 2009/10 England.
10. **The Grange Hotel**, York AA four black stars.

Famous pubs

It's such a shame that many village pubs have closed in recent years. They are full of history and tradition. Not to mention, a boarded up pub quickly becomes an eyesore. Many of our pubs are hundreds of years old and have a significant and important history.

1. **The Woolpack** at Esholt
   Esholt is a village near Bradford, in fact it's just off the Bradford to Otley road, going up Hollins Hill. The village used to be the location for Emmerdale before the village in the grounds of Harewood was built. The pub was called The Navigation, but for several years it's proudly displayed the name The Woolpack.

2. **Tan Hill Inn**
   Not only is it Britain's highest pub at 1,732 feet above sea-level, but it must also be one of the most remote. It is located on Tan Hill near the head of Arkengarthdale and on the edge of Swaledale in the northern Yorkshire Dales. The pub is near the Pennine Way and Coast to Coast paths, but most choose to drive there and what fantastic roads you have to take to get there. If there was ever a pub worth visiting just for the drive, then this is it.

3. **The Bingley Arms,** Bardsey
   The oldest pub in Britain. It has a known history that dates back to 953. Hundreds of years ago it was called The Priests' Inn. The inn was on a main route between Kirkstall Abbey and the Abbey of St. Mary's at York. In 1780 the inn was renamed and came to be known as the Bingley Arms after it was taken over by Lord Bingley.

4. **Angel Inn,** Hetton
   Under the ownership of Denis and Juliet Watkins it

became the first gastropub in the country. It caused a cultural revolution in 1985 when they did away with chips and served mangetout and fresh new potatoes with every dish. This changed the face of pub food in Britain. Hetton is a small village between Skipton and Grassington.

5. **The Minerva,** Hull
The pub, which overlooks the marina, is made up of five higgledy-piggledy rooms, one of which is the smallest snug in the UK, which accommodates just two people. The pub has a tiny theatre and Hull's only bar billiards tables. It's also famous for its giant haddock and chips. The Minerva is a one-off pub that is one of Hull's best attractions.

6. **Old Bridge Inn,** Ripponden
It has a history that dates back to 1307, but I've included this pub in my list for one simple reason - its annual pork pie competition, held every April, which attracts entrants from all over the country.

7. **The Old Silent,** Stanbury near Haworth
The inn is over 400 years old and was originally called the New Inn and then the Eagle Inn. Bonnie Prince Charlie used the inn as a hideout as he fled from Derby back to Scotland. He stayed there for several weeks, relying on the silence of locals for his safety. A reward of 30,000 guineas (about £1,000,000 in today's money) was placed on his head and eventually someone gave away his location. Soldiers descended on the pub to capture him but were spotted, allowing the young prince to escape. In recognition of the act of the villagers keeping silent, the inn was renamed The Old Silent.

Martha Grimes based one of her inspector Richard Jury novels on the inn. The book is called *The Old Silent*.

In Haworth itself you'll find the Black Bull a few yards

from the Bronte Parsonage Museum. The pub was frequented by Branwell Bronte, brother of the three famous sisters. It was in the Black Bull that Branwell drank to excess until his death from tuberculosis in 1848 at the age of 31. The pub still contains "Branwell's Chair", on which he spent many an hour brooding over his beer.

It was also voted Best Food Pub in Britain 2010 in the Great British Pub Awards.

8. **Old Hill Inn, Chapel-le-Dale, Ingleton**
Winston Churchill used to stay here on hunting, shooting and fishing holidays.

9. **Pipe and Glass Inn,** South Dalton, Beverley
Michelin Guide's Pub of the Year 2012 and also Michelin star since 2010.

10. **Shibden Mill Inn,** near Halifax
In 2011 this was voted Yorkshire's best pub in a competition run by Yorkshire's tourism agency, Welcome to Yorkshire. The George and Dragon at Hudswell was second and the Shoulder of Mutton at Kirkby Overblow was third.

If you fancy a brewery tour there are four that are worth a look:

Black Sheep Brewery, Masham
Theakston's Brewery, Masham
York Brewery
Saltaire Brewery

There's also the **Ossett Brewery** for groups.

WATERFALLS

The Yorkshire Dales is full of picturesque waterfalls. In a two or three day break to the dales you can cover all of the ones mentioned here. If you drive through upper Wharfedale above Buckden and over into Bishopdale in wet weather, then waterfalls spring up all over the place. It's brilliant and the worse the weather, the better.

1. **Aysgarth Falls**
   A triple flight of waterfalls on the river Ure in Wensleydale between Leyburn and Hawes. Total drop 30m. The falls are a product of the last ice age. Nearby Bishopdale was ground down by its glacier deeper than Wensleydale and so the river Ure had to drop down a good distance to meet up with it. The upper fall was featured in the film *Robin Hood: Prince of Thieves* starring Kevin Costner.

2. **Hardraw Fall**
   At 100 feet, it's claimed to be England's highest single drop waterfall (discounting underground waterfalls). The waterfall is just outside the tiny hamlet of Hardraw near Hawes in Wensleydale. It also featured in Costner's film of Robin Hood - remember when Maid Marian spies Robin taking a shower?

3. **Catrigg Force**
   One mile upstream from the village of Stainforth, near Settle. You reach this secluded gem via a bridleway out of the village. At Stainforth, there's also Stainforth Foss.

4. **Kisdon Force**
   This is a series of waterfalls on the river Swale just a few hundred metres downstream from the village of Keld. The word force comes from the Norse word fors or foss which means waterfall. Nearby there's also Wain Wath Falls,

Catrake Force and Currack Force.

5. **Gordale Scar waterfall**
Gordale Scar is a dramatic 100m deep limestone ravine one mile north-east of Malham. It contains two falls over which the Gordale Beck drops. In dry weather the beck can be just a trickle, but if you visit during or just after rain then the falls become quite dramatic. The setting is awesome and there's the added bonus of another beautiful waterfall called Janet's Foss a few hundred yards downstream.

6. **West Burton Falls**
This is known locally as Cauldron Falls. West Burton is a pretty village at the bottom of Bishopdale which is a tributary valley of Wensleydale. The falls are on the edge of the village and are extremely picturesque, especially after rain.

7. **Thornton Force**
You'll find this on a beautiful part of the river Twiss. It's a 14m drop and is the most famous and spectacular fall on the Ingleton Waterfalls Walk.

8. **Posforth Gill waterfall**
Posforth Gill takes water from Barden Fell to the river Wharfe via the Valley of Desolation near Bolton Abbey. You can visit this fall if you park at the Cavendish Pavilion and follow the signs for the Valley of Desolation.

9. **Whitfield Gill Force** (upstream from Mill Gill Force)
This secluded fall lies a mile from the village of Askrigg in Wensleydale. To find it walk out of the village along Mill Lane (near the church) and follow the signs for Mill Gill Force. This is another very fine waterfall. From here follow the path upstream to find Whitfield Gill Force.

10. **Mallyan Spout**
   This is a 20m high waterfall near Goathland in the North York Moors.

   Gaping Gill waterfall is 100m high, but it's underground and so not included in this list. It's formed where Beck Fell falls into the main chamber of Gaping Gill cave. It is the highest unbroken waterfall in Britain. On bank holidays local pot holing clubs set up a winch above the shaft to provide a ride to the bottom and back for members of the public.

WILDLIFE WATCHING

Great sites for watching wildlife are:

1. **Potteric Carr Nature Reserve**
   This is a 500 acre flagship wetland site of the Yorkshire Wildlife Trust. It is situated just two miles south-east of Doncaster town centre. It is the largest inland wetland in the UK outside of London.

2. **Bempton Cliffs**
   It is the best place in England to view seabirds. From April to August you'll see 200,000 puffins, gannets and guillemots. There are cliff top walks from the RSPB car park and you can also take a cruise from Bridlington.

3. **Fountains Abbey** for deer
   There's a beautiful deer park and lake at Fountains Abbey. The park is home to 500 red, fallow and sika wild deer.

4. **Snaizeholme red squirrel trail**
   The Widdale Red Squirrel Reserve near Hawes is one of only 16 areas in the UK dedicated to preserving the red

squirrel in its natural habitat. Snaizeholme is just one part of this reserve. The squirrels are provided with nuts each day from special feeders and you can see this from a viewing area. The signposted trail from the Dales Countryside Museum in Hawes is a ten mile return walk. Alternatively drive up the B6255 from Hawes to Widdale Bridge and look for the red squirrel viewpoint sign, or take the Little Red Bus from Hawes.

5. **Spurn Point** is a prime spot for watching migrating birds. It is a National Nature Reserve.

6. **Red kites at Harewood House**
The birds were released on the estate in 1999 and have bred very successfully. I drive through Harewood every week and usually see at least half a dozen without looking too hard.

7. **Malham Cove** for peregrine falcons
When the falcons take to the air the skies become eerily silent as all other birds go into hiding. Seeing the peregrines isn't guaranteed, but Malham Cove and nearby Gordale Scar are still brilliant places to visit.

8. **Cropton Forest** badger watching
Cropton Forest is run by the Forestry Commission and from May to August you can go badger watching there, though you have to book by phoning 01723 882295. The forest is near Pickering and has a campsite called Spiers House.

9. **Dearne Valley - Old Moor**
This is a great RSPB site near Barnsley.

10. **Fairburn Ings near Castleford**
Another great RSPB reserve.

Others:

There are dozens of nature reserves across the county. Too many to list, but here are a few more:

Nosterfield wetland bird reserve near Ripon
Tophill Low Nature Reserve near Watton village in the East Riding.
Staveley Nature Reserve near Boroughbridge
Mount Grace Priory is famous for its bats and stoats

Family Cycling routes

These are all completely off-road and therefore traffic free*.

1. **Trans Pennine Trail**
   The TPT is a long distance path that runs from Southport to Hornsea. It runs largely along disused railway lines and canal tow paths. It enters Yorkshire at the lofty Woodhead Pass and then passes through Dunford Bridge, Penistone, Doncaster, Selby, Hessle, Hull and Hornsea. There's also a north-south spur that links Leeds to Chesterfield via Wakefield, Barnsley, Rotherham and Sheffield. An excellent website details it all.

2. **Dalby Forest** in the North York Moors has some very family friendly routes. There are purpose built trails that are maintained by the Forestry Commission.

3. **York to Selby Cycle Route**. 15 mile totally flat route includes the York Solar System Trail. NCN route 65.

4. **The Cinder Track from Scarborough to Whitby**. This 22 mile long route follows a disused railway line through great coastal scenery, never straying more than a mile or so from the sea.

5. **The Spen Valley Greenway** follows a disused railway line between Cleckheaton and Dewsbury.

6. **Leeds-Liverpool Canal** passes through lots of quiet countryside. The canal passes through Shipley, Saltaire, Bingley, Skipton and Gargrave. These can be one way rides because the railway also links these towns.

7. **Rother Valley Country Park**. There are a couple of routes around the lakes and nature reserve. The TPT also runs through the park.

8. **Wetherby Railway Path**. Runs along a disused railway line from Thorp Arch trading estate (where there's a car park for users of the trail) to Wetherby and Spofforth. * A small section through Wetherby is along quiet lanes.

9. **Guisborough Forest and Walkway**. There's a visitor centre at Pinchinthorpe on the outskirts of Guisborough. From the visitor centre there's a disused railway line that takes you into Guisborough Forest.

10. **Great Northern Railway Trail**. At the moment this is only a very short ride between Cullingworth and Hewenden viaducts near Keighley. However there are plans to extend the trail along the disused railway line to Denholme, Thornton and Queensbury. If and when this happens this will be a great family ride through Bronte country.

Art galleries

Most are free and make for an interesting afternoon out.

1. **The Hepworth Wakefield**
   "One of the finest contemporary art museums in Europe" according to *The Independent*.
2. **MIMA** - Middlesbrough Institute of Modern Art
3. **Yorkshire Sculpture Park**, West Bretton, Wakefield
4. **Leeds City Art Gallery**
5. **The Henry Moore Institute**, Leeds
6. **York City Art Gallery**
7. **Ferens Art Gallery**, Hull
8. **Graves Art Gallery**, Sheffield
9. **Ruskin Collection**, Millennium Gallery, Sheffield
10. **1853 Gallery**, Salts Mill, Saltaire. Permanent exhibition of Bradford born David Hockney.

Biggest and best museums

1. **Magna**, Rotherham
2. **National Media Museum**, Bradford *
3. **National Railway Museum**, York *
4. **Royal Armouries Museum**, Leeds *
5. **Eden Camp**, near Malton
6. **York Castle Museum**
7. **National Coal Mining Museum for England**, Overton, Wakefield *
8. **Yorkshire Air Museum**, York
9. **Yorkshire Museum**, York
10. **Thackray Museum**, Leeds *

* free entry

Great days out for children

1. **Forbidden Corner**, near Middleham
2. **Canon Hall Farm**, near Barnsley
3. **Magna**, Rotherham
4. **The Deep**, Hull
5. **Yorkshire Wildlife Park**, Doncaster
6. **Flamingo Land**, near Malton
7. **Lightwater Valley**, near Ripon
8. **Aerial Extreme**, Bedale and Sheffield
9. **Go Ape**, Dalby Forest
10. **Diggerland**, Castleford

Gardens in North and East Yorkshire

1. **RHS Harlow Carr**, Harrogate (Valley Gardens in Harrogate are also nice and you can walk from there to Harlow Carr)
2. **Fountains Abbey** and **Studley Royal**, near Ripon
3. **Thorp Perrow Arboretum** near Bedale
4. **Scampston Hall and Walled Garden**, five miles east of Malton
5. **Burnby Hall Gardens**, near Pocklington
6. **Sledmere House and Garden**, 7 miles north-west of Driffield
7. **Burton Agnes Hall and Gardens**, midway between Driffield and Bridlington
8. **Constable Burton Hall and Gardens**, near Leyburn
9. **Newby Hall and Gardens** near Ripon
10. **Himalayan Gardens**, Grewelthorpe, near Ripon

Other great gardens:

Breezy Knees Gardens, Warthill, York
Parcevall Hall Gardens in Wharfedale near Burnsall
Stillingfleet Lodge Gardens, York
Yorkshire Lavender west of Malton
Wolds Way Lavender east of Malton
Sutton Park, Sutton-on-the-Forest, 8 miles north of York
Beningbrough Hall and Gardens, 8 miles north-west of York
Duncombe Park, Helmsley and Helmsley Walled Garden
Goddards Garden, York

South and West Yorkshire have some great gardens. They include:

Brodsworth Hall and Gardens, five miles north-west of Doncaster
Wentworth Castle Gardens, Stainborough, near Barnsley
Harewood House Garden
Bramham Park
Sheffield Botanical Gardens
York Gate, Adel, Leeds

Finest stately homes and country houses in North and East Yorkshire

1. **Castle Howard**, near York
2. **Burton Agnes Hall and Gardens**, midway between Driffield and Bridlington
3. **Burton Constable Hall**, between Hull and Hornsea
4. **Sledmere House**, near Driffield
5. **Newby Hall and Gardens**, near Ripon
6. **Ripley Castle**, near Harrogate
7. **Sewerby Hall and Gardens**, near Bridlington
8. **Beningbrough Hall**, near York
9. **Kiplin Hall**, near Northallerton
10. **Scampston Hall** near Malton

Other grand houses are:

Nunnington Hall, near York
Fairfax House, York
Treasurer's House, York
Newburgh Priory Estate, Coxwold, near Thirsk
Sion Hill Hall near Thirsk
Norton Conyers near Ripon
Markenfield Hall near Ripon
Duncombe Park nearHelmsley
Ormesby Hall near Middlesbrough

FINEST STATELY HOMES AND COUNTRY HOUSES IN WEST AND SOUTH YORKSHIRE

1. **Harewood House**, near Leeds
2. **Temple Newsam**, near Leeds
3. **Nostell Priory**, near Wakefield
4. **Bramham Park**, near Leeds
5. **Brodsworth Hall and Gardens**, near Doncaster
6. **Shibden Hall**, Halifax
7. **Oakwell Hall**, Birstall, Batley
8. **Lotherton Hall**, Leeds
9. **Cannon Hall**, Cawthorne, near Barnsley
10. **East Riddlesden Hall**, Keighley

There's also:

Cusworth Hall near Doncaster.
Wentworth Woodhouse near the village of Wentworth.
Its east front is the longest country house facade in
Europe. It's 185m long. Unfortunately the house is not
open to the public, however, the parkland surrounding it is.

Best castles to visit

Yorkshire doesn't have any large, well preserved castles like Windsor or Caernarfon, but many of the castles that we do have are still worth a visit.

1. **Bolton Castle**
   In the heart of Wensleydale between Leyburn and Aysgarth Falls. This is a very well preserved castle that dates back to 1399. Lots to see and do include birds of prey displays.

2. **Ripley Castle**
   700 year old castle three miles from Harrogate owned and lived in by the Ingilby family.

3. **Richmond Castle**
   Constructed from 1071 as part of the Norman Conquest. Now owned by English Heritage. Originally called Riche Mount which meant "the strong hill".

4. **Middleham Castle**
   Built from 1190 it sits in a lovely location in the village of Middleham in Wensleydale. Childhood home of Richard III. Owned by English Heritage.

5. **Conisbrough Castle**
   The 12th Century keep is very well preserved and new floors and roof were put in during the 1990s. Owned by English Heritage.

6. **Pickering**
   The motte and bailey earthworks date from the 11th Century and the stone castle that replaced the original wooden one from the 12th Century.

7. **Helmsley Castle**
   Dates from the 1180s. Much remains of the east tower, but little else. The site also contains a Tudor mansion. Owned by English Heritage.

8. **Scarborough Castle**
   Dates from the 1150s. Great views of Scarborough North Bay.

9. **Clifford's Tower**
   Set on a tall mount in Old York, it is virtually all that remains of York Castle which was built by William the Conqueror.

10. **Skipton Castle**
    Built in the early 14th Century. Very well preserved, though quite small.

There's also:

Knaresborough Castle
Sandal Castle
Pontefract Castle
Skipsea Castle
Spofforth Castle

Best abbeys and priories to visit

The Yorkshire monasteries were amongst the most powerful and wealthiest in the country. They owned vast tracts of land and dominated the landscape until their destruction by King Henry VIII in the 1530s. Yorkshire has some of the most famous abbeys in the country including Fountains Abbey, Whitby and Rievaulx.

1. **Fountains Abbey and Studley Royal**
   Near Ripon. Now a World Heritage Site owned by the National Trust. Cistercian abbey dating from the 12th Century. They are the largest abbey ruins in the country and the site also contains very fine Georgian water gardens. The adjoining deer park adds to the attraction. The seven bridges walk around the deer park is excellent if you are feeling fit.

2. **Whitby Abbey**
   The first abbey on this site was founded in 657 AD by Oswy, King of Northumbria. It was laid waste by the Vikings in the late 800s. A second abbey was built in stone at the end of the 11th Century by Reinfrid who was a soldier of William the Conqueror. After the Norman invasion he became a monk and travelled north to what was now called Hwitebi. The great location of the abbey overlooking the port was the inspiration behind Bram Stoker's novel Dracula.

3. **Bolton Abbey**
   In Wharfedale near Ilkley. Majestic ruins overlooking the river Wharfe just within the boundary of the Dales National Park. The location is wonderful and there are beautiful river walks from the ruins. Definitely the busiest location in the dales because of its proximity to Leeds and Bradford, so if you can visit mid-week. Founded by the Augustinian order in 1154.

4. **Kirkstall Abbey**
   In Leeds next to the river Aire. After Fountains, Kirkstall is one of the most complete Cistercian abbeys in the country. It was founded in 1152.

5. **Rievaulx Abbey**
   Cistercian abbey founded in 1132 in a peaceful and beautiful small wooded valley near Helmsley. One of the most complete and atmospheric of England's abbey ruins.

6. **Jervaulx Abbey**
   Cistercian abbey founded in 1156. In a very tranquil setting near the village of East Witton in Wensleydale. There's a very nice tea-room that contains a brilliant model made by Derek Shaw of how the abbey used to be.

7. **Mount Grace Priory**
   The best preserved Carthusian priory in Britain. Founded in 1398. Near Osmotherley in North Yorkshire.

8. **Roche Abbey**
   Founded in 1147 by Cistercian monks. Near Maltby in South Yorkshire. Capability Brown landscaped the surroundings in the 1770s.

9. **Byland Abbey**
   Founded as a Savigniac house in 1134 but brought within the Cistercian order in 1147. It was one of the largest abbeys in England and by the late 12th Century Byland, Fountains and Rievaulx were described as "the three shining lights of the north".

10. **Easby Abbey**
    A Premonstratensian abbey founded in 1152. In a very nice location by the river Swale in Richmond.

Others:

Kirkham Priory
Monk Bretton Priory
York St. Mary's
Gisborough Priory

CATHEDRALS, MINSTERS AND CHURCHES

I'm not at all religious, but I do marvel at and enjoy visiting grand churches. Yorkshire has some of the most amazing in the world.

1. **York Minster**
   The largest gothic cathedral in northern Europe.

2. **Beverley Minster**
   Definitely one of the finest Gothic churches in Europe. Often described as the best non-cathedral church in England.

3. **Selby Abbey**
   It is one of the few surviving abbey churches from the medieval period and although it's not a cathedral it has the size and the beauty of one.

4. **Ripon Cathedral**
   The crypt located beneath the central tower dates from 672. The west front is 13th Century and the seven light east window is 14th Century.

5. **Wakefield Cathedral**
   It has the tallest spire in Yorkshire, at 247 feet. Built in the 14th Century it is one of only four remaining bridge chapels in England.

6. **Cathedral Church of St Peter and St Paul, Sheffield**
   Built in 1430 using the perpendicular gothic style. In 1914 it was raised from town church to cathedral status.

7. **Rotherham Minster**
   Sir Nikolaus Pevsner, who wrote *The Buildings of England* series, described Rotherham Minster as "the best perpendicular church in the country".

8. **Doncaster Minster**
   Built between 1854 and '58 after the medieval church was destroyed by fire in 1853.

9. **Holy Trinity Church, Hull**
   The Guinness Book of Records notes the 700 year old church as England's largest parish church in area.

10. **Bradford Cathedral**
    A small, but beautiful 500 year old cathedral.

Others:

Halifax Minster
Leeds Parish Church
Dewsbury Minster
Bolton Abbey Church
Howden Minster

Best National Trust sites

1. **Fountains Abbey**, Ripon
2. **Brimham Rocks**, near Ripon
3. **Beningbrough Hall and Gardens**, near York
4. **Nunnington Hall**, near York
5. **Ormesby Hall**, Middlesbrough
6. **Treasurer's House**, York
7. **Mount Grace Priory**, near Northallerton
8. **East Riddlesden Hall**, Keighley
9. **Hardcastle Crags**, Hebden Bridge
10. **Rievaulx Terrace**, near Helmsley

Best English Heritage sites

1. **Brodsworth Hall and Gardens**, near Doncaster
2. **Rievaulx Abbey**, near Helmsley
3. **Richmond Castle**
4. **Whitby Abbey**
5. **Helmsley Castle**
6. **York Cold War Bunker**
7. **Conisbrough Castle**
8. **Pickering Castle**
9. **Scarborough Castle**
10. **Middleham Castle**

Other English Heritage sites in Yorkshire are:

Kirkham Priory
Clifford's Tower, York
Aldborough Roman Site
Roche Abbey
Spofforth Castle
Byland Abbey

Scenic and heritage railways

1. **Settle to Carlisle railway**
   The most scenic railway in England. From Settle the line passes by the three peaks of Pen-y-Ghent, Ingleborough and Whernside. It crosses the Ribblehead viaduct and heads up through Dentdale, Garsdale and the Eden Valley. There is a regular scheduled service and you can begin your journey at Leeds or Skipton. On certain days there are steam services.

2. **North Yorkshire Moors Railway**
   Brilliant. It's like stepping back in time. The steam trains run from Pickering to Whitby with stops at Goathland and Grosmont. Goathland was Aidensfield in Heartbeat and its railway station became Hogsmeade in the first Harry Potter film.

3. **Esk Valley line**
   This links Middlesbrough to Whitby. It passes through Danby, Egton and Lealholm, which are arguably Yorkshire's prettiest villages.

4. **Wensleydale Railway**
   This steam railway runs for 16 miles from Leeming Bar to Redmire, passing through Bedale and Leyburn. The train gives great views of Wensleydale. At Redmire you can visit Bolton Castle and Aysgarth Falls.

5. **Keighley and Worth Valley Railway**
   Famous for its use in the *Railway Children* film.

6. **Embsay and Bolton Abbey Steam Railway**
   Embsay is a village near Skipton. The line is four miles long and the picturesque priory ruins beside the river Wharfe are a one and a half mile walk from the Bolton Abbey station.

7. **Kirklees Light Railway**
Steam trains run along this four mile mile between Shelley and Clayton West near Huddersfield.

8. **Elsecar Heritage Railway**
This is South Yorkshire's only preserved line. Steam and diesel locomotives run along the one mile line from the Elsecar Heritage Centre near Barnsley.

9. **Middleton Railway**
It's the world's oldest continuously working railway. Steam engines run along a one mile line in Hunslet, Leeds.

10. **Derwent Valley Light Railway**
This half mile long track is part of the Yorkshire Museum of Farming known as Murton Park at Murton near York.

LONG DISTANCE WALKS

Yorkshire is a walkers' paradise. Spectacular scenery and pretty villages, it's no wonder that the county has so many long-distance walks. Here are the ten longest.

The longest ones are national trails and cross two or more counties. For these, I've quoted the complete trail length and not the length of the section that passes through Yorkshire.

All of the walks are supported by official bodies such as the national parks authorities and county councils. The walks are therefore clearly marked and there are websites and guide books available that describe the routes.

1. **Pennine Way** 268 miles
From The Naggs Head pub in Edale in Derbyshire to The Border Inn at Kirk Yetholm just inside the Scottish border. A very long section of the trail passes through Yorkshire from Hebden Bridge in the south to Tan Hill in the north.

2. **Trans Pennine Trail** 215 miles
The trail runs coast to coast between Southport and Hornsea.

3. **Coast to Coast** 192 miles
From St. Bees in Cumbria to Robin Hood's Bay. It was devised by Alfred Wainwright.

4. **Cleveland Way** 109 miles
The trail runs between Helmsley and Filey around the North York Moors National Park.

5. **Yorkshire Wolds Way** 79 miles
From Hessle to Filey Brigg.

6. **Dales Way** 78 miles
Ilkley to Bowness-on-Windermere.

7. **Ribble Way** 71 miles
The trail largely follows the course of the river Ribble. The route begins in Longton near Preston and ends at the source of the Ribble at Gayle Moor near Ribblehead.

8. **Ebor Way** 70 miles
Starts at Helmsley and finishes at Ilkley. It passes through the Howardian Hills Area of Outstanding Natural Beauty and takes in York.

9. **Nidderdale Way** 53 miles
This is a circular walk that runs along both sides of the Nidderdale valley between Ripley and Scar House reservoir.

10. **Bronte Way** 43 miles
From Birstall to Padiham in Lancashire.

LONGEST RIVERS

1. **Ure** 74 miles
   From its source in upper Wensleydale to the point where it changes its name to the river Ouse. This point is Cuddy Shaw Reach near Linton-on-Ouse.

2. **Swale** 73 miles
   Its source is at the confluence of Birkdale Beck and Great Sleddale Beck. It flows through Keld, Muker, Reeth, Richmond, Catterick and Helperby. It joins the river Ure just below Myton-on-Swale.

3. **Derwent** 72 miles
   It rises on Fylingdales Moor, flows through the Vales of Pickering and York and joins the Ouse at Barmby on the Marsh.

4. **Aire** 71 miles
   Rises at Malham Tarn, flows underground to Aire Head near Malham, flows through Gargrave, Skipton, Bradford and Leeds. At Castleford it meets the Calder and at the village of Airmyn it joins the Ouse.

5. **Don** 70 miles
   It rises in the Peak District on Great Grains Moss and flows eastwards through Penistone, Sheffield, Rotherham, Conisbrough and Doncaster. At Goole it joins the Ouse.

6. **Wharfe** 60 miles
   Its source is at Beckermonds in Langstrothdale. It flows through Kettlewell, Grassington, Burnsall, Bolton Abbey, Ilkley, Wetherby and Tadcaster. Near Cawood it joins the river Ouse.

7. **Nidd** 59 miles
   Rises at Nidd Head Spring on the slopes of Great Whernside. It's dammed three times to form the reservoirs of Angram, Scar House and Gouthwaite. It then flows through Pateley Bridge and Knaresborough. It joins the Ouse at Nun Monkton.

8. **Tees** 55 miles
   The Tees is actually 85 miles long, but only 55 miles of it is in Yorkshire. Before the reorganisation of the historic English counties it marked the boundary between County Durham and Yorkshire. Since the reorganisation the upper part is in County Durham.

9. **Ouse** 52 miles
   The river is formed from the river Ure at Cuddy Shaw Reach near Linton-on-Ouse. It then flows through York, Selby and Goole before joining the river Trent at Trent Falls near the village of Faxfleet to form the Humber estuary.

10. **Calder** 45 miles. The source is Heald Moor near Todmorden. It flows through Sowerby Bridge, Brighouse, Dewsbury and Wakefield. At Castleford it joins the river Aire.

Highest peaks in the Yorkshire Dales National Park

Parts of the national park are in Cumbria. This list only includes peaks within Yorkshire.

1. **Whernside** 736m
   Yorkshire's highest peak sits next to the Ribblehead viaduct not far from Ingleton. Before the boundary changes in 1974, Mickle Fell at 788m, was the highest point in Yorkshire. It's now in county Durham.

2. **Ingleborough** 723m
The most popular of all the hills in the dales. Overlooks the town of Ingleton.

3. **Great Shunner Fell** 716m
This is the highest point in Wensleydale. The Pennine Way passes across its summit on the way from Hawes to Keld.

4. **Great Whernside** 704m
This mountain sits above Kettlewell in Wharfedale. It forms the watershed between Wharfedale and Nidderdale.

5. **Buckden Pike** 702m
This peak stands above the village of Buckden at the head of Wharfedale.

6. **Pen-y-ghent** 694m

7. **Plover Hill** 680m
An area of moorland north of Pen-y-ghent.

8. **Lovely Seat** 675m
5km north of Hawes, it's part of the high ground which separates Wensleydale from Swaledale.

9= **Great Knoutberry Hill** 672m
Located near Dent at the heads of Ribblesdale, Dentdale and Wensleydale. The Cumbria/North Yorkshire border runs over the hill.

9= **Rogan's Seat** 672m
Not too far from Tan Hill in upper Swaledale. It has a reputation as being the most boring 2000 foot hill in England.

Places of geological interest

Yorkshire and North Yorkshire in particular, is full of geological wonders. They might not be the size of the Grand Canyon or Niagara Falls, but they are still brilliant, mostly free and surrounded by glorious countryside. If you've never been to Brimham Rocks or How Stean Gorge, then get your map out and make a day of it. For the brave and adventurous, visit Gapping Gill on a bank holiday weekend and get winched to the bottom. It's an experience you'll never forget and it only costs a tenner.

The carboniferous limestone from which the Yorkshire Dales are made gives rise to caves, gorges and waterfalls. It's the geology of the Dales that make them so beautiful.

1. **Gaping Gill cave**
   A 100m deep pothole on the southern side of Ingleborough mountain. It's the largest known cavern in Britain. Fell Beck falls into it creating Britain's highest unbroken waterfall. The potholing clubs that set up the winch system on bank holiday weekends also floodlight the cave to create a truly awe-inspiring scene.

   The walk to the cave from the village of Clapham isn't bad either. The footpath passes through a nature reserve, past Ingleborough Cave and through the impressive gorge of Trow Gill.

2. **Malham Cove**
   The whole area around the village of Malham is brilliant. The carboniferous limestone bedrock has given rise to a very dramatic landscape. Malham Cove is an 80m high and 300m wide cliff that lies on the mid-craven fault 1km north of Malham. Millions of years ago an earthquake pushed the land north of the fault upwards to create the cove.

   On the west side of the cove are 416 steps that take you to the top of the cove where you will find a great view and a vast expanse of classic limestone pavement.

Just behind the cove is Watlowes Valley (a dry steep sided gorge) that is also worth exploring. 1km to the east of the cove is Gordale Scar, described below.

3. **Brimham Rocks**

This is a large area of gritstone tors, some standing 30m high, in Nidderdale near Pateley Bridge. Brimham rocks is owned by the National Trust. It's a brilliant place, especially for kids who like climbing and scrambling and the views of Nidderdale are superb.

4. **How Stean Gorge**

The steep sided chasm in upper Nidderdale is almost 1km in length and 20m deep. You follow winding pathways and explore tunnels and caves. There's also a via ferrata which is a network of beams, ladders and cables that allow you to walk along the vertical sides of the gorge.

5. **Gordale Scar**

This is a dramatic limestone ravine 1.5km north east of Malham. It contains two waterfalls and has overhanging cliffs over 100m high. As I head into it I always expect giant scary dinosaurs to come walking out of it - it's a weird place.

If you are driving to Malham from Gargrave, just as you pass Kirkby Malham Primary School you get an amazing view of the entrance to Gordale Scar on your right and Malham Cove to the left.

If you visit Gordale Scar make sure you don't miss Janet's Foss waterfall downstream from it.

6. **White Scar Cave**

Britain's largest show cave. It contains the enormous Battlefield Cavern. White Scar Cave is just outside Ingleton.

7. **Ingleborough Cave**

The half kilometre long cave is on the south side of

Ingleborough mountain. The cave is a 30 minute walk from the village of Clapham.

8. **Stump Cross Caverns**
   Another cave system located in the Yorkshire Dales on the road between Pateley Bridge and Grassington.

9. **Hardraw Force**
   At 30m, it's England's highest single drop waterfall. It's set at the end of a gorge within the grounds of the Green Dragon Inn in the hamlet of Hardraw near Hawes.

10. **Bempton cliffs**
    The hard chalk cliffs at Bempton are over 100m high in places and run for about 10km from Flamborough Head to Filey. The cliffs are home to 200,000 birds during the summer and according to the RSPB are the best place in England to view seabirds. You can walk along the cliff top or take a boat trip from Bridlington on certain days.

There's also:

The Hole of Horcum
An enormous natural amphitheatre in the North York Moors next to the Pickering to Whitby road. It's 130m deep and three quarters of a mile across. You can walk around and in it.

Troller's Gill
A limestone gorge near Appletreewick in Wharfedale. It's about 300m long and just a few metres wide. Children will have seen it in the TV show *Roger and the Rottentrolls* (which is also shot at Brimham Rocks). The gorge lies behind Parceval Hall Gardens which are certainly worth a visit.

Aysgarth Falls
Perhaps the most picturesque falls in the country. Located in upper Wensleydale near Leyburn.

ADRENALINE-FUELLED DAYS OUT

1. **Gaping Gill cave**
   On certain bank holidays local pot holing clubs set up a winch system to allow members of the public to visit this truly awe-inspiring place.

2. **Bungee jumping** off the Middlesbrough Transporter Bridge. This iconic metal structure carries cars and people across the river Tees. It opened in 1911 and serves as a reminder to the region's great industrial past. For the very brave, the bungee jump takes place from a height of well over 200 feet.

3. **The Abyss at Magna**, Rotherham
   The only indoor extreme sports centre in the UK. It offers the Awesome Foursome which utilises the breathtaking facilities and structure of the former steel works:
   250 foot zip wire
   Abseil 150 feet into the Abyss
   150 foot parachute simulator
   The world's only indoor bungee jump, just 150 feet!

4. **Zorbing**
   This is where you are strapped into a giant inflatable ball and left to roll at great speed down a hill. There's a place called Spheremania in Leeds - they've even got two-seater zorbs. You can also zorb at the Rother Valley Country Park.

5. **Aerial Extreme**, Bedale and Sheffield
   Tree-top walkways, swings and zip wires.
   Go Ape at Dalby Forest offers a similar adventure.

6. **White water rafting** on the Washburn river near Pateley Bridge. This is offered by Xperience Adventure. For 30 days each year the dam at the head of the river is opened to produce white water conditions.

7. **How Stean Gorge via ferrata**
   How Stean is a brilliant limestone gorge near Pateley
   Bridge. It has one of only two via ferratas in England. Via
   ferrata literally means "iron way" and is a network of metal
   ladders, cables and beams set into the gorge walls.

8. **Learn to sail or windsurf** at the Yorkshire Dales Sailing
   Club based at Grimwith reservoir near Grassington.

9. **Learn to surf**
   Fluid Concept Surf School at Scarborough.

10. **Hot air ballooning**
    Offered by Go Ballooning with launch sites all over
    Yorkshire.

Places with Literary Connections

1. **Haworth**
   The village is almost as famous as Stratford-Upon-Avon as
   a place for literary pilgrimage. It's where the Bronte sisters
   lived and wrote their novels. The nearby abandoned
   farmhouse called Top Withens is thought to be the
   inspiration for Emily's *Wuthering Heights*. Their home, the
   old parsonage, is now the Bronte Parsonage Museum.

2. **Thirsk**
   Alf Wight, the real life James Herriot lived and worked in
   the town for over 50 years. His house and surgery are
   preserved as they were in the 1940s and are open as the
   James Herriot Centre. Thirsk is called Darrowby in his
   books and The Golden Fleece Inn on the market square is
   Herriot's Drovers' Arms. The Three Tuns Hotel, also on the
   market square was Alf Wight's favourite watering hole.

3. **Whitby**
   In 1897 Bram Stoker wrote *Dracula* whilst staying at Ravenscar. Whitby was the setting for his book.

   Bram Stoker got some of his inspiration for *Dracula* after staying in Whitby in 1890. In Stoker's book, Dracula is shipwrecked off the coast of Whitby. He comes ashore in the guise of a black dog and wreaks havoc on the town.

4. **Halifax**
   Daniel Defoe wrote most of *Robinson Crusoe* at The Rose and Crown in Cheapside in Halifax. "I was born in the year 1632 in the city of York" is the opening of the novel.

5. **Malham Cove**
   Charles Kingsley was inspired to write *The Water Babies* after a trip to Malham in 1863. In the book he describes the cove as "that awful cliff".

6. **Sutton-on-the-Forest**
   Laurence Sterne wrote *The Life and Opinions of Tristram Shandy, Gentleman* whilst living and working in the village. Sterne was the village's vicar. The novel was published in nine volumes, the first two appearing in 1759 and seven others following over the next ten years.

7. **Northallerton**
   Charles Dickens wrote much of *Nicholas Nickleby* whilst staying at The Old Fleece Inn on the high street. Dickens also stayed at The Black Swan in York and The Morritt Arms in Greta Bridge while he researched the novel. Dickens wished to highlight the hardship and cruelty inflicted by certain Yorkshire schools on their boys.

8. **Croft-on-Tees**
   Lewis Carroll and *Alice in Wonderland*. Carroll's real name was Charles Lutwidge Dodgson. His father was the rector of St. Peter's Church in Croft for 25 years. Historians think

that the Cheshire Cat was inspired by a carving in St. Peter's. Carroll was 11 years of age when he came to live at Croft. It's thought that much of *Alice in Wonderland* is set in and around the rectory and church.

9. **Greenhow Hill** (near Pateley Bridge)
Rudyard Kipling's book of short stories titled *Life's Handicap* - chapter 17 is called "On Greenhow Hill". Rudyard's grandfather, Joseph Kipling, was the minister at Greenhow Methodist Chapel. Rudyard is known to have visited the village. There is Kipling's Cottage next door to what used to be The Miners' Arms. Of course, Rudyard Kipling is famous for writing *The Jungle Book*.

10. **Hubberholme** in upper Wharfedale
J. B. Priestley (perhaps best remembered for his stage play *An Inspector Calls*) called Hubberholme "one of the smallest and pleasantest places in the world" and he asked for his ashes to be buried in the churchyard. Dick Hudson's near Eldwick and the moors behind it, were also a favourite place of Priestley's.

William Wordsworth married Mary Hutchinson at All Saints Church in the village of Brompton by Sawdon which is 8 miles west of Scarborough.
    Wordsworth visited and wrote poems about Malham Cove and Gordale Scar in 1819.

PLACES ASSOCIATED WITH THE BRONTE SISTERS

The Brontes are the world's most famous literary family. To have three literary geniuses in one family is unique. All three sisters died young and the family's story is just as fascinating as the books they wrote. Many of the places and characters described in their books were based on places and people they knew in their own lives. A great website to visit to learn more is haworth-village.org.uk

1. **74 Market Street,** the Parsonage of Thornton village near Bradford. This is where they were all born. Charlotte in 1816, Emily in 1818 and Anne in 1820.

2. **The Parsonage at Haworth**
   Home to the Brontes from 1820 to 1861. Charlotte's novel *Jane Eyre* (1847), Emily's *Wuthering Heights* (1847) and Anne's *The Tenant of Wildfell Hall* (1848) were written in the parsonage.

3. **Haworth Church**
   Charlotte and Emily are buried in a vault inside the church. Charlotte died in 1855 aged 38 and Emily died in 1848 aged 30.

4. **Scarborough**
   In January 1849 Anne was diagnosed with tuberculosis. On 24 May she and Charlotte travelled to Scarborough in the hope that the sea air might alleviate Anne's symptoms. Sadly, Anne died on the 28th. She was buried in St. Mary's churchyard on Castle Hill overlooking Scarborough Bay. She was just 29 (even though her gravestone says she was 28). Anne is the only member of the Bronte family not buried at Haworth.

5. **Top Withens**
   Top Withens is an old abandoned farmhouse high on the moors above Haworth. It's now a ruin. It was last inhabited in 1926. Top Withens has been associated with *Wuthering Heights*, the Earnshaw home in Emily's novel. However, the buildings never bore any resemblance to the house she described. More likely, Emily had in mind the situation of Top Withens when she described the setting for *Wuthering Heights*.

The walk from Haworth to the farmhouse is an excellent one.

6. **Oakwell Hall near Birstall**
   The Hall was the main location for the recent ITV adaptation of *Wuthering Heights*. Charlotte Bronte visited the hall regularly and it was featured as Fieldhead, the home of the heroine in Charlotte's novel, *Shirley.*

7. **Norton Conyers near Ripon**
   It's a medieval manor house and was visited by Charlotte in 1839. It's thought to have been the inspiration for Charlotte's Thornfield Hall in the novel *Jane Eyre*. The discovery in 2004 of a blocked staircase connecting the first floor to the attic which is clearly described in the novel aroused world-wide interest. The legend of a mad woman confined to the attic a century before is thought to have given Charlotte the idea for the mad Mrs Rochester.

8. **Roe Head School and Blake Hall at Mirfield**
   Charlotte attended Roe Head School from January 1831 to June 1832. In July 1835 she returned as teacher and stayed there until May 1938. Emily went to Roe Head School in July 1935 but only stayed there for three months. In 1935 Anne enrolled at Roe Head School. She left in 1937. Roe Head featured in Charlotte's novel *Shirley*.

   Roe Head was a boarding school for girls and it opened in 1830. In 1956 Roe Head School became the Verona Fathers, a college for men pursuing a life of priesthood. In 1990 the school once again changed ownership and became Holly Bank School.

   From 1839 to 1840 Anne worked as governess to the Ingham family at Blake Hall. She was dismissed for being unable to control the young Inghams. Her novel *Agnes Grey* describes her experiences.

   The Blake Hall estate is now a modern housing estate.

The area is largely encompassed by Blake Hall Road and Blake Hall Drive. There are two cul-de-sacs called Bronte Way and Bronte Grove.

9. **Wycoller Country Park**

Wycoller Hall, now a ruin, is thought to be Ferndean Manor in *Jane Eyre*.

10. **Cowan Bridge**

When they moved to Haworth in 1820, the Bronte family consisted of Patrick and his wife Maria and their six children, Maria, Elizabeth, Charlotte, Branwell, Emily and Anne. In 1821 the mother Maria died of cancer, aged 38. Patrick struggled to raise six children on his own and so in 1824 sent Maria, Elizabeth, Charlotte and Emily to the Clergy Daughters' School at Cowan Bridge. However, they only stayed a year because the school was filthy and unhealthy. Maria and Elizabeth died of consumption not long after returning to Haworth. The conditions at the school were largely to blame.

Cowan Bridge is near Kirkby Lonsdale.

Some other places with a Bronte connection:

Ponden Hall near Stanbury is thought to be Thrushcross Grange, the home of the Linton family in *Wuthering Heights*.
Red House Museum, Gomersal near Leeds. Red House is Briarmains in Charlotte's novel *Shirley*. Charlotte frequently visited the house to see her friend Mary Taylor.
In 1809 Patrick began his curacy at Dewsbury.
In 1812 Patrick and Maria were married at Guiseley Church.
Their first child, Maria, was baptised at Hartshead in 1814.
Elizabeth was born in Hartshead, near Huddersfield.
In 1841 Charlotte became a governess for the White family who lived at Upperwood House in Rawdon.

Places associated with James Herriot and All Creatures Great and Small.

Alf Wight was born in Sunderland in 1916. He qualified at the Glasgow Veterinary College and then moved to Yorkshire. In 1970 Alf's first book, *If Only They Could Talk*, was published under the pseudonym James Herriot.

Alf used to write his books whilst watching television. On one night he was watching a football game involving Birmingham City. One player, Jim Herriot, Birmingham's best player and a fellow Scot caught his attention. From then on all of his stories as a Yorkshire vet were told by James Herriot. Alf died of cancer in 1995 at his home in Thirlby.

1. **Thirsk**. He worked for the now famous Kirkgate Surgery in Thirsk This is now The World of James Herriot. In his novels Thirsk becomes the fictional town of Darrowby.

2. **St. Mary Magdalene Church** in Thirsk – married Joan here in November 1941.

3. **The Wheatsheaf** pub in Carperby is where they spent their honeymoon.

4. **Sutton Bank**. Alf liked to walk here and described the view from the top as the best view in the world.

5. **Askrigg** in Wensleydale doubled for the fictional Darrowby in the TV series *All Creatures Great and Small*. See if you can spot Skeldale House on the main street, opposite and just below the church. The King's Arms Hotel in Askrigg became the Drovers' Arms in the TV series.

6. **The Richmondshire Museum**, Richmond
   The original set of the interior of the Skeldale House surgery is now located at the museum. (The living room

and the dispensary are on display at The World of James Herriot in Thirsk).

7. **Unnamed road between Feetham in Swaledale and Langthwaite in Arkengarthdale.**
   Parts of the opening title sequence in the TV series were filmed on this road, including where the car goes through the ford. Surrender Bridge was used as the water splash.

8. **Malton**. The location for the 1974 film *All Creatures Great and Small* that starred Simon Ward and Anthony Hopkins.

9. **Wensleydale and Swaledale**. Where most of the rural locations were filmed.

10. **The Red Lion Inn** in Langthwaite. The inside and outside were used in several episodes.

PLACES ASSOCIATED WITH JAMES COOK

Perhaps Yorkshire's greatest son. He is renowned the world over as an explorer, pioneering navigator and preventer of scurvy.

Since his death in 1779 Cook's life and achievements have been recognised and commemorated across the globe.

All over North Yorkshire, from Middlesbrough to Great Ayton; Redcar to Marske and Staithes to Whitby there are places with Cook connections. This area is known as Captain Cook Country.

1. **Marton near Middlesbrough -** Cook's birthplace. Here you'll find:
(i) The Captain Cook Birthplace Museum in Stewart Park. It opened in 1978 on the 250th anniversary of Cook's birth.

A granite urn just to the south of the museum marks the site of his birthplace cottage.

(ii) In St. Cuthbert's Parish Church there is a memorial stained glass window to Cook. The church holds an annual service of thanksgiving for Cook's life on the Sunday nearest his birthday which is the 27th of October.

2. **Great Ayton**

When Cook was a child his family moved to Aireyholme Farm near Great Ayton and it was here that he was schooled and worshipped. In or near Great Ayton you'll find:

(i) The Captain Cook Schoolroom Museum. In Cook's time this was known as the Postgate School and Cook studied there from 1736 to 1740.

(ii) The James Cook sculpture on High Green.

(iii) The 12th Century All Saints Church. As a boy, Cook worshipped here with his family. Cook's siblings are buried in the churchyard. His parents are buried in Marske-by-the-sea.

(iv) Cook Obelisk erected in 1827 on Easby Moor, overlooking the village of Great Ayton.

(v) Memorial garden. This is the site where Cook's father built a family home in 1755. The cottage was dismantled and moved to Australia in 1934. A granite obelisk stands in the garden and it is constructed from stone taken from Point Hicks, the first land sighted by Cook in Australia.

3. **Whitby**

Cook left Staithes and moved to Whitby in 1747 and began an apprenticeship in the merchant navy, transporting coal along the north-east coast. Cook stayed in Whitby until 1755 when he volunteered as an ordinary seaman in the Royal Navy.

There's the Captain Cook Memorial Museum in the house where he lodged.

Statue of Captain Cook on Whitby's West Cliff.

Two of Cook's ships, *Resolution* and *Endeavour*, were built in Whitby. Cook captained *HMS Endeavour* on his first voyage of discovery. He captained *Resolution* on his second and third voyages.

A smaller, replica *Endeavour* takes passengers around Whitby harbour and out to sea.

4. **Staithes**
Captain Cook and Staithes Heritage Centre.

For a year and a half from 1745, Cook was an apprentice to William Sanderson, who owned a grocery shop in the village. Legend has it that it was in Staithes that he first felt the allure of the sea.

5. **Middlesbrough** contains many memorials to Cook. There's the James Cook University Hospital and a primary school and shopping square bare his name.

6. **Hawaii.** The site where he was killed in Hawaii is marked by a white obelisk built in 1874. About 25 square feet of land around it is chained off and has been given to the UK. A nearby town is called Captain Cook. NASA commemorated Captain Cook in naming two of its space shuttles after his ships, *Endeavour* and *Discovery*.

7. **Cook crater** is on the Moon.

8. **James Cook University** in Townsville in North Queensland, Australia.

9. **Mount Cook** is the highest summit in New Zealand.

10. **The Cook Islands, Cook Strait and Cook Inlet.**
In the Pacific Ocean.

MUSIC, FILM
AND TV

Pop Groups

1. **Def Leppard**
   Formed in Sheffield in 1977. They are one of the world's biggest selling bands. They've sold over 65 million albums. *Hysteria* and *Adrenalize* have topped the album charts in both the UK and the US.

2. **Arctic Monkeys**
   Formed in 2002 in Sheffield. Their debut album, *Whatever People Say I Am, That's What I'm Not* (2006) became the fastest-selling debut album in British music history. It sold over 360,000 copies in its first week. As of 2011 the band has released four albums, all of which have reached number 1 in the UK album chart.

3. **The Beautiful South**
   Formed in Hull in 1988 by Paul Heaton and Dave Hemingway. The band broke up in 2007 after releasing ten studio albums. Two of these reached number 1 in the UK and six others made the top 10. The band also had six top ten singles.

   Paul Heaton had founded The Housemartins along with Stan Cullimore in 1983. Other band members included Norman Cook who went on to become Fatboy Slim. The band split in 1988. Two top 10 albums and two top ten singles.

4. **Embrace**
   Post Britpop band from Bailiff Bridge near Brighouse. Formed in 1990. Five top 10 albums between 1998 and 2006, three of them reaching number 1. Also six top 10 singles, including the England 2006 World Cup song *World at Your Feet*.

5. **Human League**
   Formed in Sheffield in 1977. Phil Oakley is the lead vocalist and songwriter. They have had four albums and nine singles in the UK top ten. 1981 was the band's biggest year - the year saw the release of the album Dare and the single *Don't You Want Me?*

6. **Pulp**
   Formed in Sheffield in 1978, however, they didn't gain prominence until the mid 1990s. Jarvis Cocker is the lead singer. The band has released seven studio albums and two of them reached number one in the UK. They've also had four top 10 singles.

7. **Kaiser Chiefs**
   Indie rock band from Leeds that formed in 1996. Named after the South African football club Kaizer Chiefs. As of 2011 the band has released four top 10 studio albums, one of them reaching number 1. They've also had five top 10 singles, with *Ruby* reaching the top spot.

8. **ABC**
   Formed in Sheffield in 1980. Between 1981 and 1991 the new romantic band had a great deal of chart success including a number 1 album and three top 10 singles.

9. **Everything But The Girl**
   Formed in Hull in 1981. Made up from Tracey Thorn and Ben Watt who were students at Hull University. The duo took their band name from a well known furniture shop called Turners' in Hull. The store once had a window sign that read, "for your bedroom needs, we sell everything but the girl". The last part of that slogan was later added to the shop's main signage.

   EBTG released 11 studio albums between 1984 and 1999. Three of these reached the top 10. Also four top 10 singles.

10. Whitesnake

Founded in Middlesbrough in 1978 by David Coverdale after his departure from Deep Purple. In 1987 the single *Here I Go Again* topped the American charts. *Is This Love* reached number 2. David Coverdale was born in Saltburn-by-the-Sea in 1951.

Other groups from Yorkshire include:

Soft Cell

Synthpop band who came to prominence in 1981 with the number 1 single *Tainted Love*. The band consists of vocalist Marc Almond and instrumentalist David Ball. The pair formed the band while they were studying at Leeds Polytechnic.

Smokie

The group that eventually became known as Smokie was formed by three school chums at St Bede's Grammar School in Bradford. During the mid 1970s the group had a string of hit singles. Though their popularity in the UK declined in the 1980s the group continued to have hit albums and singles in Europe. Russian president Putin is a massive fan.

Sisters of Mercy formed in Leeds
The Cult are from Bradford
New Model Army - Bradford
Heaven 17 - Sheffield
The Cribbs - Wakefield
Gang of Four - Leeds
Shed Seven - York

One Direction also has two tykes. They are Zayn Malik from Bradford and Louis Tomlinson from Doncaster.

Kimberley Walsh from Bradford is part of Girls Aloud.
Melanie Brown from Leeds is part of The Spice Girls.
Tom Bailey, who founded the Thompson Twins was born in Halifax.

SINGERS AND SONGWRITERS

1. **Chris Rea**
   Born in Middlebrough in 1951. He's sold over 30 million albums worldwide. His albums *The Road to Hell* and *Auberge* have topped the UK albums chart. He wrote *Fool (If You Think It's Over)* which was a hit for Elkie Brooks. His song *Driving Home for Christmas* is one of the most popular Yuletide songs.

2. **Robert Palmer**
   Born in Batley in 1949. Died 2003. His 1986 single *Addicted to Love* reached number 1 in America and number 5 in the UK. The following year he won the Grammy Award for Best Male Rock Vocal Performance for the song. In 1989 he won a second Grammy for *Simply Irresistible*.

3. **Corinne Bailey Rae**
   Born in Leeds in 1979. In 2006 her debut album reached number 1 in the UK. It reached number 4 in the US album chart and went on to win the Grammy for album of the year.

4. **Tony Christie**
   Born Anthony Fitzgerald in 1943 in Conisbrough. Best known for the singles *Is This The Way To Amarillo?*, *I Did What I Did For Maria* and *Avenues and Alleyways*. *Is This The Way To Amarillo* was re-released in 2005 to raise money for Comic Relief. It was number 1 for seven weeks. His album; *The Definitive Collection* also reached number 1. In 2011 Christie released his 19th studio album.

5. **Joe Cocker**
   Born in Sheffield in 1944. Best known for *Up Where We Belong*; a song from the 1982 film *An Officer and a Gentleman*, which he sang with Jennifer Warnes. The song won an Oscar and a Grammy.

6. **Gareth Gates**
   Born in Bradford in 1984. Runner-up in the first series of the ITV show Pop Idol in 2002. Four number 1 singles followed.

7. **Ed Sheeran**
   Born in Halifax in 1991. His debut album released in 2011 reached number 1 in the UK selling over one million copies. In 2012 Ed won two Brit awards - best British breakthrough act and British male solo artist.

8. **Kiki Dee**
   Born Pauline Matthews in Bradford in 1947. Best known for her 1976 duet with Elton John entitled *Don't Go Breaking My Heart*. The song was a number 1 hit in both the UK and the US.

9. **Arthur Brown**
   Born in Whitby in 1948. "I am the God of hellfire". Best known for his number 1 single *Fire* released in 1968.

10. **Vic Reeves**
Has topped the UK singles chart with *Dizzy*. His version of *Born Free* also made the top 10.

Other musicians from Yorkshire:

Lesley Garrett
Born in Thorne near Doncaster in 1955. Opera singer. For a time she was the principal soprano at English National Opera. In 2002 she was awarded the CBE for her services to music. In 2004 she finished third in the first series of *Strictly Come Dancing*.

Frederick Delius
Born in Bradford in 1862. Died in 1934. Composer.

John Barry
Born John Barry Prendergast in York in 1933. Died 2011. He composed the soundtracks for 12 Bond movies between 1962 and 1987. He also wrote scores for the films *Midnight Cowboy, Born Free, Dances with Wolves* and *Out of Africa*. His film scores won many awards including five Oscars.

Geoff Love
Born in Todmorden in 1917. Died 1991. Composer, bandleader and trombonist. Laurie London and The Geoff Love Orchestra topped the American charts in 1958 with the gospel song *He's Got the Whole World in His Hands*. He directed and arranged music for many artists including Johnny Mathis, Des O'Connor, Judy Garland, Marlene Dietrich, Gracie Fields and Randy Crawford. He became well known to the public through his TV appearances with Max Bygraves in the 1970s.

FILM ACTORS

1. **Charles Laughton**
   Born 1899 in Scarborough. Died 1962. Won the Oscar for best actor in 1933 for his role in *The Private Life of Henry VIII*. Nominated for best actor two other times.

2. **Sir Ben Kingsley**
   Born 1943 in Snainton near Scarborough. Best actor Oscar winner in 1982 for his portrayal of Gandhi. Oscar nominated two other times.

3. **James Mason**
   Born 1909 in Huddersfield. Died 1984. Oscar nominated three times for *The Verdict* (1982), *Georgy Girl* (1966) and *A Star Is Born* (1954).

4. **Sir Patrick Stewart**
   Born 1940 in Mirfield. Played Captain Jean-Luc Picard in *Star Trek: The Next Generation* and Professor Charles Xavier in the *X-Men* films.

5. **Dame Judy Dench**
   Born 1934 in York. Starred in the TV series *A Fine Romance* from 1981 to '84 and *As Time Goes By* from 1992 to 2005. Since 1995 she has played M in the James Bond films. In 1998 she won the Oscar for best supporting actress for her portrayal of Elizabeth I in *Shakespeare in Love*.

6. **Sir Tom Courtenay**
   Born 1937 in Hull. Twice Oscar nominated. Came to prominence in the 1960s for his performances in *The Loneliness of the Long Distance Runner* (1962), *Billy Liar* (1963) and *Dr. Zhivago* (1965). Twice Oscar nominated for his roles in *Dr. Zhivago* and *The Dresser* (1983).

7. **Malcolm McDowell**
Born 1943 in Horsforth. Perhaps best known for playing the lead in *A Clockwork Orange* (1971).

8. **Brian Blessed**
Born 1936 in Goldthorpe near Barnsley. Probably best known for that voice. Played PC "Fancy" Smith in the BBC drama series *Z-Cars* from 1962-65. Portrayed Caesar Augustus in *I, Claudius*, also for the BBC. On stage he starred in Andrew Lloyd Webber's *Cats* during the original London production. In film he played Prince Vultan in *Flash Gordon* (1980) and Robin Hood's dad in Kevin Costner's film *Robin Hood: Prince of Thieves* (1991).

9. **Tom Wilkinson**
Born 1948 in Leeds. Twice Oscar nominated for his roles in *In The Bedroom* (2001) and *Michael Clayton* (2007). He also starred in *The Full Monty* (1997).

10. **Sean Bean**
Born 1959 in Sheffield. Best known for playing Colonel Richard Sharpe in the ITV series *Sharpe* and for playing Boromir in the *Lord of the Rings* trilogy. He has featured in many blockbuster films including *Patriot Games* (1992) alongside Harrison Ford, *Goldeneye* (1995), *Ronin* (1998) and *Troy* (2004).

Peter O'Toole, although Irish, was possibly born in Leeds in 1932. Apparently he doesn't know if he was born in Leeds or Connemara in Ireland.

Other actors from Yorkshire include Brian Glover, Brian Rix, Mark Addy (from *The Full Monty*), Georgina Helen Henley (from *The Chronicles of Narnia*) and Richard Griffiths.

TV ACTORS

1. **Mollie Sugden**
   Born 1922 in Keighley. Died 2009. Best known for portraying saleswoman Mrs Slocombe in *Are You Being Served?* from 1972 to 1985.

2. **Wendy Richard**
   Born 1943 in Middlesbrough. Died 2009. She played Miss Brahms in *Are You Being Served?* and Pauline Fowler in *Eastenders*.

3. **Diana Rigg**
   Born in Doncaster in 1938. Best known for her role in the 1960s series *The Avengers*, in which she played secret agent Mrs Emma Peel. She also played Countess Teresa di Vicenzo in the 1969 James Bond film *On Her Majesty's Secret Service*.

4. **John Simm**
   Born 1970 in Leeds. John is one of the most popular TV actors of the last decade. He played Sam Tyler in *Life On Mars*. He also played The Master in *Doctor Who* and starred in the drama series *State of Play*.

5. **Rodney Bewes**
   Born 1937 in Bingley. Played Bob Ferris in the BBC sitcom *The Likely Lads* (1964-66) and its sequel *Whatever Happened to the Likely Lads?* (1973-74).

6. **Gordon Kaye**
   Born 1941 in Huddersfield. Played Rene Artois in BBC's *'Allo, 'Allo!* from 1982-92.

7. **Dominic West**
   Born 1969 in Sheffield. Best known for his role as

Detective Jimmy McNulty in the American TV police drama *The Wire* that ran from 2002 to 2008.

8. **Adrian Edmondson**
Born in Bradford in 1957. Came to prominence in the early 1980s and is best known for his roles in TV comedies *The Young Ones* (1982-84) and *Bottom* (1991-2003).

9. **Jack Shepherd**
Born in 1940 in Leeds. Best known for playing Detective Superintendent Charles Wycliffe in *Wycliffe*.

10. **Timothy West**
Born 1934 in Bradford. Film, stage and television actor. He became well known in 1975 for playing Edward the Seventh in the TV series of the same name. He also starred in the ITV comedy *Brass* between 1982 and 1990. He's married to Prunella Scales.

Other stars of television:

Julian Barrett
Born 1968 in Leeds. Co-writer and star of *The Mighty Boosh*.

Brian Mosley
Born 1931 in Leeds. Died 1999. Played Alf Roberts in *Coronation Street*.

Maureen Lipman
Born 1946 in Hull.

Helen Worth
Born in Ossett in 1951. Plays Gail Platt in *Coronation Street*.

Ian Kelsey
Born in York in 1966. Has been in *Emmerdale* and *Casualty*.

TV PRESENTERS

1. **Sir Michael Parkinson**
   Born in Cudworth, near Barnsley, in 1935.

2. **Richard Whiteley**
   Born in Bradford in 1943. Died 2005. Hosted *Countdown* for 23 years from 1982 until his death.

3. **Jeremy Clarkson**
   Born in Doncaster in 1960. He trained as a journalist on the *Rotherham Advertiser*. Presenter of *Top Gear* since 1988.

4. **Jeremy Paxman**
   Born in Leeds in 1950. Presenter of *Newsnight* since 1989 and *University Challenge* since 1994.

5. **John Craven**
   Born in Leeds in 1940. Worked on the *Harrogate Advertiser* and then the *Yorkshire Post*. Hosted John Craven's *Newsround* from 1972 to 1989. He fronted *Countryfile* from 1988 to 2009.

6. **Alan Titchmarsh**
   Born in Ilkley in 1949. Hosted *Pebble Mill at One*, *Gardener's World* and *Groundforce*. Since 2007 he's had his own chatshow.

7. **James Martin**
   Born in Malton in 1972. His father was head chef at Castle Howard and this is where James first learned to cook. As well as presenting *Saturday Kitchen* and writing a motoring column for the *Mail On Sunday*, he also owns The Leeds Kitchen restaurant in Clarence Dock.

8. **Roy Castle**
Born 1932 in Scholes, near Holmfirth. Died 1994. In the mid 1960s he starred in the BBC television show *The Roy Castle Show*. From 1972 until 1994 he hosted *Record Breakers*.

9. **John Noakes**
Born in Shelf near Halifax in 1934. Co-hosted *Blue Peter* from 1965 until 1978. He remains the show's longest serving presenter.

10. **Gabby Logan**
Born 1973 in Leeds. Daughter of footballer Terry Yorath.

Others:

Harry Corbett
Born 1918 in Bradford. Died 1989. Created Sooty and Sweep.
Matthew Corbett
Born 1948 in Guiseley. Son of Harry. Took over Sooty from his father in 1976.
Hannah Hauxwell
Born 1926 in North Yorkshire. Farmer in the high Pennines who was the subject of several ITV documentaries.
Selina Scott
Born 1951 in Scarborough. *News at Ten, BBC Breakfast Time, Wogan*.
John Kettley
Born 1952 in Halifax. Weatherman.
Chris Moyles
Born 1974 in Leeds. Radio 1 presenter.
Paul Daniels
Born 1938 in Middlesbrough. Magician.
Alex Zane
Born 1979 in Leeds.

COMICS

1. **Ernie Wise**
   Ernest Wiseman was born in Leeds in 1925. He died in 1999. Ernie first met Eric Morecambe in 1940. Gradually they formed a close friendship and in 1941 they began their comedy double act.

2. **Michael Palin**
   Born in Sheffield in 1943. Helped write and starred in the ground breaking Monty Python sketch shows.

3. **Frankie Howerd**
   Born in York in 1917. Died in 1992. Fellow comedian, Barry Cryer, described Howerd's career as a series of comebacks, spanning six decades.

4. **Vic Reeves**
   Born James Roderick Moir in Leeds in 1959. Best known for his double act with Bob Mortimer.

5. **Bob Mortimer**
   Born in Middlesbrough in 1959. As a teenager he had football trials for Middlesbrough. Arthritis put paid to a career in football, so Bob became a solicitor. He met and started working with Vic Reeves in 1986.

6. **Roy "Chubby" Brown**
   Born Royston Vasey in 1945. Grangetown near Middlesbrough. His blue humour means that he rarely appears on television. However, he has a strong fan base and it's claimed that he performs to over 350,000 people each year.

   His real name was used as the name of the fictional town in the comedy TV show *The League of Gentlemen*. In the show he made a number of cameo appearances as the foul-mouthed mayor.

7. **Leigh Francis**
   Born in Leeds in 1973. Best known for creating the Channel 4 show *Bo' Selecta* and the character Keith Lemon who has hosted a number of shows including *Celebrity Juice*.

8. **Barry Cryer**
   Born in Leeds in 1935. One of Britain's best comedy writers. He's written for many comedians including Dave Allen, Jasper Carrott, Tommy Cooper, The Two Ronnies and Morecambe and Wise.

9. **Charlie Williams**
   Born in Royston near Barnsley in 1927. Died 2006. He was Britain's first well known black comedian. He was also a professional footballer, playing 151 times for Doncaster Rovers between 1948 and 1959.

10. **The Chuckle Brothers**
    Barry Elliott born 1944 and Paul Elliott born 1947 in Rotherham. The Chuckle Brothers won *Opportunity Knocks* in 1967 and *New Faces* in 1974. They are best known for their BBC children's comedy show called *ChuckleVision* which has run since 1987.

Other notable comics from Yorkshire are:

Maureen Lipman
Born in Hull in 1946
Marti Caine
Born in Sheffield in 1944. Died from cancer in 1995
Bobby Knutt
Born in Sheffield in 1945.
Jeremy Dyson
Born in Leeds in 1966. Co-writer and actor from the *League of Gentlemen*.

FAMOUS FILMS SET IN YORKSHIRE

1. **Room at the Top**
   1959 starred Simone Signoret and Laurence Harvey. Set in the late 1940s in the fictional Yorkshire towns of Dufton and Warnley. Most of the film was shot in Halifax. The film was nominated for six Oscars and won two. The film came 32nd on the BFI's 1999 list of the best British films ever. It was followed by the sequel *Life at the Top* in 1965.

2. **Calendar Girls**
   2003 starred Helen Mirren and Julie Walters. True story about the members of the Rylstone Women's Institute. Locations throughout Wharfedale were used.

3. **The Full Monty**
   1997 starred Robert Carlyle and Tom Wilkinson. Six unemployed steel workers form a male striptease act. Set in Sheffield. The screenplay was written by Simon Beaufoy from Keighley (he also wrote the screenplay for *Slumdog Millionaire*).

4. **The Railway Children**
   1970 starred Jenny Agutter, Dinah Sheridan and Bernard Cribbins. Lionel Jeffries who directed the film used the Keighley and Worth Valley Railway and its station at Oakworth as the backdrop to the film. The house "Three Chimneys" is in Oxenhope and the Bronte Parsonage was used as the location for Doctor Forrest's surgery.

5. **Kes**
   1969 film by Ken Loach based on the novel *A Kestrel for a Knave* by the Barnsley born author Barry Hines. The film was set in Barnsley and the school used was the St. Helens School in Athersley. In 1999 the British Film Institute voted Kes the 7th greatest British film ever.

6. **The Damned United**
   2009 film about Brian Clough's tenure as manager of
   Leeds United. Starred Michael Sheen and Timothy Spall.

7. **Billy Liar**
   1963 starred Tom Courtenay and Julie Christie. A story
   about William Fisher, a working-class 19 year old from the
   fictional town of Stradhoughton in Yorkshire. Much of the
   film was shot in Bradford.

8. **This Sporting Life**
   1963 starred Richard Harris. The film tells the story of
   rugby league player Frank Machin in Wakefield. The film
   was shot in Wakefield, Halifax and Leeds. In 1999 the BFI
   voted *This Sporting Life* the 52nd best British film ever.

9. **Brassed Off**
   1996 starred Ewan McGregor, Tara Fitzgerald and Pete
   Postlethwaite. The film was set in the fictional town of
   Grimley in the mid 1990s. The film was shot largely in
   Grimethorpe and the soundtrack for the film was recorded
   by the Grimethorpe Colliery Band. In 1994 the European
   Union's study of deprivation named Grimethorpe as the
   poorest town in the country. The 1981 census recorded
   44% of Grimethorpe's workers as miners. The film is set
   against the closure of the village's pit and the break up of
   its brass band.

10. **Brideshead Revisited**
    (2008). Just like the TV serial the film was shot at Castle
    Howard. The film starred Emma Thompson.

Films that have used locations in Yorkshire:

1. **Robin Hood: Prince of Thieves** (1991).
   Kevin Costner's Robin Hood fought Little John on Aysgarth Falls. He also took a shower at Hardraw Force near Hawes.

2. **Harry Potter and the Philosopher's Stone** (2001).
   Goathland station was turned into Hogsmeade.

3. **Harry Potter and the Deathly Hallows (part 1)** (2010) used Malham Cove.

4. **The King's Speech** (2011). At the start of the film the Duke of York gives the closing speech at the 1925 Empire Exhibition, supposedly at Wembley Stadium. The scenes were actually shot at Elland Road football stadium and Grattan Stadium (home of Bradford Bulls).

5. **The Dark Crystal** (1982) fantasy film by Jim Henson also used Malham Cove and Gordale Scar.

6. **Monty Python and the Holy Grail** (1974) also used Malham Cove.
   The Meaning of Life used Ilkley Moor and Lister Park in Bradford.

7. **Atonement** (2007) starring Keira Knightley and James McAvoy was shot on Redcar beach.

8. **Elizabeth** (1998) starring Kate Blanchett was shot at York Minster.

9. **Chariots of Fire** (1981). Hales Bar in Harrogate and the National Railway Museum at York for the railway station scenes.

10. **Omen III: The Final Conflict** (1981). The finale was shot at Fountains Abbey.

Television series shot in Yorkshire

1. **Emmerdale**
First broadcast in 1972 as *Emmerdale Farm*. The nearby village was known as Beckindale. Originally, filming took place in the village of Arncliffe in Littondale which is a tributary valley of Wharfedale. From 1976 the village of Esholt near Bradford was used. The original *Emmerdale Farm* buildings are near the village of Leathley and Home Farm is Creskeld Hall. From 1998 a purpose built village set built on the Harewood estate has been used. Butlers Farm is really Brookland Farm which is in the nearby village of Eccup. Otley is used as the fictional market town of Hotten. Indoor scenes are filmed mostly in Yorkshire Television's Emmerdale Production Centre on Kirkstall Road in Leeds.

2. **Last of the Summer Wine**
Ran from 1973 to 2010. It was set and filmed in and around Holmfirth. Every episode was written by Roy Clarke.

3. Heartbeat
Police drama set in 1960s Yorkshire. It ran from 1992 to 2010. Goathland in the North York Moors was used as the fictional village of Aidensfield. The series was originally based on the Constable books written by former policeman Peter Walker/Nicholas Rhea.

4. All Creatures Great and Small
Seven series were made between 1978 and 1990. The series were based on the books written by James Herriot (real name Alf Wight). Christopher Timothy played Herriot. The original shows also starred Robert Hardy and Carol Drinkwater. The Wensleydale village of Askrigg doubled as the fictional Darrowby.

5. Rising Damp
Ran from 1974 to '78 and starred Leonard Rossiter (Rupert Rigsby), Frances de la Tour (Miss Jones), Richard Beckinsale (Alan) and Don Warrington (Philip). A feature film was made in 1980. The exact setting was never made clear, but it was made in Leeds and the setting is generally accepted as being somewhere in Yorkshire.

6. Open All Hours
Four series between 1976 and '85. Starred Ronnie Barker and David Jason. Written by Roy Clarke. The shows were shot in Balby which is a suburb of Doncaster.

7. A Touch of Frost
15 series were made between 1992 and 2010. Starred David Jason. Although set in the fictional south midlands town of Denton most of it was filmed in Leeds, Wakefield, Pontefract and Castleford.

8. **In Loving Memory**
   Five series starring Thora Hird and Christopher Beeny were made between 1979 and 1986. The setting was the fictitious Lancashire town of Oldshaw. The actual location for filming was Bramham near Leeds and Luddendon near Halifax.

9. **Oh no, it's Selwyn Froggit**
   Three series were made between 1974 and '77. The show starred Bill Maynard and outdoor filming took place in Skelmanthorpe and Elvington.

10. **Only When I Laugh**
    Four series were made by Yorkshire Television between 1979 and '82. Starred James Bolan, Peter Bowles, Christopher Strauli and Richard Wilson and was set in a ward in an NHS hospital. The title is the answer to the question "Does it hurt?"

Other TV series:

Fat Friends (2000-05) Shot in Leeds.
The Royal (2003-11) Shot in Scarborough and St. Luke's Hospital, Bradford.
The Gaffer (1981-83) Filmed in Leeds.
Dalziel and Pascoe (1996-2007)
At Home With the Braithwaites (2000-03) Leeds.
Follyfoot (1971-73) Harewood estate near Leeds.
Hadleigh (1969-76) Farnley Hall near Otley and Creskeld Hall near Bramhope.
Roger and the Rottentrolls (1996-2000) Brimham Rocks.
The Bounder (1982-83)
How's Your Father (1979-80)
Billy Liar (1973-74)

Television dramas shot in Yorkshire

1. **The Beiderbecke trilogy**
   Three serials called *The Beiderbecke Affair* (1985), *The Beiderbecke Tapes* (1987) and *The Beiderbecke Connection* (1988). Starred James Bolan and Barbara Flynn whose characters taught in a rundown comprehensive school in Leeds.

2. **Brideshead Revisited**
   Made in 1981 by Granada Television. Based on the novel of the same name written by Evelyn Waugh in 1945. Starred Jeremy Irons and Anthony Andrews and of course Castle Howard.

3. **Red Riding Trilogy**
   The three feature length episodes aired in 2009. They were based on David Peace's *Red Riding Quartet* which were published between 1999 and 2002. The serial starred Sean Bean, Mark Addy, David Morrissey and Paddy Considine. Various locations across Bradford were used.

4. **Mansfield Park**
   This two hour long ITV drama based on Jane Austen's book was filmed at Newby Hall near Ripon. The film starred Billy Piper.

5. **This is England '86 and This is England '88**
   The two Channel 4 drama serials were shown in 2010 and 2011. Much of the filming for '86 took place in the Gleadless Valley area of Sheffield. Park Hill Flats in Sheffield were used for '88.

6. **Harry's Game**
   This three part serial was made in 1982 and about Captain Harry Brown, a soldier sent undercover to Northern Ireland

to infiltrate the IRA and arrest the murderer of a British cabinet minister. Set in Belfast, Yorkshire Television filmed most of the scenes in a now-demolished housing district in Burley, which was adjacent to their Leeds Studios.

7. **Band of Gold**
   There were three series of this drama shown on ITV between 1995 and '97. Written by Leeds girl Kay Mellor. Starred Geraldine James and Barbara Dickson. Set around Lumb Lane in the Manningham area of Bradford.

8. **Wuthering Heights**
   Oakwell Hall was the main location for the 2009 ITV adaptation of Emily Bronte's novel. Starred Tom Hardy and Charlotte Riley.

9. **A Woman of Substance**
   This three part mini-series was broadcast on Channel 4 in 1985. It starred Jenny Seagrove and Liam Neeson and was based on the novel by Barbara Taylor Bradford. It was filmed at Broughton Hall near Skipton, Ricmond, Aysgarth Falls and Brimham Rocks.

10. **The Railway Children**
    There were three TV adaptations even before the 1970 film was thought about. Just like the film, the 1968 TV serial starred Jenny Agutter and the Keighley and Worth Valley Railway.

FOOD AND DRINK

Famous food companies/
brands founded in Yorkshire

1. **Terry's**

   In 1823 Joseph Terry became a partner in a York confectionery business owned by Robert Berry. The company was called Terry and Berry and had a shop in St. Helen's Square. (The Terry name is still on the front of the building). Berry died and Terry was left to expand the business himself. He became well known for cakes, comfits, sugared sweets, candied peel, marmalade and medicated lozenges. Joseph died in 1850 and the company was taken over by his son, Joseph Terry junior. By now the company was called Joseph Terry and Sons. In 1926 the massive Terry's factory was built. Terry's All Gold was first produced in 1930 and the Chocolate Orange a year later. In 1993 the company was taken over by Kraft, which closed down the factory in 2005. Production of Terry's products moved to plants in Europe.

2. **Rowntree's**

   In 1862 Henry Isaac Rowntree purchased a cocoa and chocolate business in York. In 1869 he was joined by his brother, Joseph. They were both tea-total Quakers and they promoted chocolate drinks as an alternative to alcoholic ones. Fruit Pastilles were introduced in 1881. Fruit Gums came along in 1893. Tooty Frooties and Jelly Tots followed. In the 1930s the company launched Kit Kat, Aero, Smarties, Polos, Black Magic and Dairy Box. Munchies came along in 1957 and After Eights in 1962. In 1969 Rowntree's merged with the Halifax company Mackintosh to form Rowntree's Mackintosh Ltd. In 1988 Rowntree's was bought by Nestle.

   Mackintosh was started by John Mackintosh in 1890. His wife Violet developed a recipe for toffee which blended traditional, brittle English butterscotch with soft, American caramel. They sold the toffee as Mackintosh's Celebrated Toffee. It was a huge success and Mackintosh's became a very large company. Halifax became known as "Toffee Town". Mackintosh's went on to develop brands such as Quality Street, Rolo, Caramac and Toffee Crisp.

3. George Bassett's and Co

Simply known as Bassett's. Founded by George Bassett in Sheffield in 1842. The company's most famous product, Liquorice Allsorts, were created after George's death in 1899. The mascot of Bassett's, Bertie Bassett, was created in 1929. Bassett's are also famous for producing Jelly Babies, Wine Gums and Dolly Mixtures. In 1989 Bassett's was taken over by Cadburys.

The story of how Liquorice Allsorts were invented is an interesting one. In 1890 a Bassett's salesman called Charlie Thompson was visiting a wholesaler in Leicester with a case full of different liquorice sweets. Each sweet in turn was rejected. Collecting his sample boxes together, Charlie clumsily dropped them and the sweets made a jumbled mess on the floor. The wholesaler looked at this and thought the mixed up sweets were a better idea and placed an order.

4. Thorntons

Founded by Joseph William Thornton in 1911 in Sheffield. Joseph wanted to open the nicest sweet shop in Sheffield. He had another job which he couldn't afford to give up so he made his 14 year old son, Norman, the manager of the shop. The shop took £20 a week and this convinced Joseph to give up his job and open a second shop.

Joseph died in 1919 and his two sons took over the business. In 1923 they opened two more shops in Sheffield and in 1926 another two. One of these was in Rotherham. By 1938 there were 35 shops in 18 towns across northern England. By 1967 the company had nearly 90 shops. This figure grew to nearly 400 by 2010. Sadly, in 2011 Thorntons announced that it would have to close between 120 and 180 of its shops.

5. Fox's Biscuits

Founded in 1853 by Michael Spedding who opened a small confectionery shop in the centre of Batley. Michael retired in 1897 and the company passed to his son-in-law, Fred Ellis Fox. In 1927 the company moved to premises on the outskirts of Batley, the present site. Well known products include Rocky, Classic, Echo and in the seasonal market, Creations. Since 1977 Fox's Biscuits has been part of Northern Foods plc.

6. Seabrook Crisps

Founded in 1945 by Charles Brook in Bradford. The name came about because of an error in a photo-processing shop. Instead of writing C. Brook, a clerk wrote Seabrook.

7. Aunt Bessie's

Founded in Hull in 1995. The company began as Tryton Foods, which from 1974 made and sold frozen Yorkshire puddings to Butlins Holiday Camps. Aunt Bessie's is now the world's largest brand of frozen baked Yorkshire puddings. They put a million Yorkshire puddings on UK plates every week.

8. Farrah's of Harrogate

The company was founded in 1840 by John Farrah. The Original Harrogate Toffee was designed to clear the palate of the horrid taste of Harrogate's Sulphur Water, which was famous for its healing properties. Farrah's is still based in Harrogate and now makes over 250 products. Farrah's shop in Harrogate must be the best sweet shop in Yorkshire.

9. Yorkshire Wensleydale Creamery

The famous cheese has been made at the Wensleydale Creamery in Hawes to time-honoured traditional recipes for more than a hundred years. It's made using milk from local farms, where the cows graze limestone meadows that are rich in wild flowers, herbs and grasses. It's this herbage that gives the milk and hence the cheese its distinctive flavour.

Beware, not all Wensleydale cheese is made in Wensleydale. Some of it is made in Lancashire and the Wensleydale Creamery isn't happy about this. The Creamery is trying to get protected status for the cheese. This will mean that manufacturers outside Wensleydale will not be able to call their produce Yorkshire Wensleydale.

Wensleydale cheese was first made by Cistercian monks who settled in the valley in the 12th Century, first at Fors and then at Jervaulx. When the monastery was dissolved in 1540, local farmers continued making the cheese.

10. Harry Ramsden's

The world's most famous fish and chip brand. In 1928 Harry Ramsden began selling fish and chips from a small striped wooden hut beside a tram stop on the outskirts of Guiseley. It was a very popular spot as the main roads out of Bradford and Leeds going towards Wharfedale converged there. Within three years Harry opened his fish and chip "palace" on the same site, modelled on London's Ritz hotel. It was the biggest fish and chip restaurant in the world. Sadly, that famous restaurant closed down in 2011 but today there are 35 outlets throughout the UK and even ones in Saudi Arabia, Australia, Hong Kong and Disney World in Florida.

Others:

Bettys and Taylors of Harrogate

Bettys was established in 1919 by Frederick Belmont from Switzerland. After studying baking and confectionery he accidentally found himself in Bradford. He liked the countryside and clean air and so decided to stay. He opened his first Bettys Cafe Tea Room in Harrogate. Bettys was an instant success and Belmont opened more branches in towns across Yorkshire. Today there are Bettys in Harrogate, York, Ilkley and Northallerton. In 1962 Bettys bought Taylors of Harrogate.

After 90 years, the identity of Betty still remains a mystery.

Taylors of Harrogate were established in 1886 by Charles Taylor. The company is famous for Yorkshire Tea and Taylors of Harrogate Coffee.

Henderson's Relish

Henry Henderson of Sheffield began making his own spicy sauce in the late part of the 19th Century. It's similar to Worcester sauce but doesn't contain anchovies, so it's suitable for vegetarians. The sauce is still made in Sheffield.

Brymor ice-cream

Made at High Jervaulx Farm in Wensleydale. Made using milk from Guernsey cows. The farm has an ice cream parlour that sells 35 flavours of ice cream.

KP Snacks

KP began in Rotherham in 1853 as Kenyon and Son selling sugar, confectionery, jams and pickles. Later, the company became known as Kenyon, Son and Craven and then as KP, which stands for Kenyon Produce. KP Nuts were introduced in 1953.

FAMOUS SWEETS

Yorkshire has given the world some of its best loved sweets.

1. **Pomfret Cakes** - Liquorice sweets more commonly called Pontefract cakes today. First made in Pontefract by apothecary George Dunhill in 1760. Liquorice Pomfret cakes made without sugar were first made in the early 1600s as medicines. Dunhill hit upon the idea of adding sugar to the liquorice and sell them as sweets.

2. **Fruit Pastilles** - introduced by Rowntree's of York in 1881, although they were made in Tyneside. Before then, manufacture of gums and pastilles had been a French monopoly.

3. **Fruit Gums** - came along in 1893; another Rowntree's invention.

4. **Liquorice Allsorts** - invented in 1899 by George Bassett and Co. Ltd of Sheffield. The mascot, Bertie Bassett, was invented in 1926.

5. **Jelly Babies** - launched by Bassett's in 1918 to celebrate the end of World War One. They were originally called Peace Babies. Shortage of raw materials during World War 2 stopped production, but in 1953 they made a comeback, this time known as jelly babies.

6. **Dolly Mixtures** - made by Bassett's since the 1920s.

7. **Polos** - introduced by Rowntree's of York in 1948. The hole was introduced in 1955.

8. **Tooty Frooties** - invented by Rowntree's in 1963.

9. **Jelly Tots** - invented by Rowntree's in 1967.

10. **Yorkshire Mixtures** - by Joseph Dobson and Sons Ltd of Elland.

FAMOUS CHOCOLATES

Terry's, Thorntons, Rowntree's and Macintosh's were all founded in Yorkshire.

Terry's can trace its roots back to 1823 when Joseph Terry became a partner in the confectionery business of Robert Berry. In 1993 Terry's was taken over by Kraft Foods. The York factory was closed in 2005 and production of Terry's chocolates moved overseas.

Joseph William Thornton opened his first sweet shop in Sheffield in 1911. Thorntons famous Easter eggs began in 1922. Thorntons Special Toffee came out two years later. In the 1950s Thorntons started making its Continental Assortment chocolates. In 1948 production of Thorntons confectionery moved from Sheffield to Derbyshire.

Rowntree's was founded in York in 1862 by Henry Isaac Rowntree. In 1869 he was joined by his brother Joseph.

John Macintosh and his wife Violet bought a pastry shop in Halifax in 1890 and began making toffee. Violet developed a recipe which blended traditional English brittle butterscotch with American soft caramel and came up with Macintosh's Celebrated Toffee.

In 1969 Macintosh's merged with Rowntree's to form Rowntree Macintosh, which was itself taken over by Nestle in 1988.

1. **Terry's All Gold** - first made in 1930 at the famous Terry's factory off Bishopthorpe Road in York.

2. **Terry's Chocolate Orange** - introduced in 1931.

3. **Kit Kat** - introduced by Rowntree's in 1935. Originally it was called Rowntree's Chocolate Crisp and sold for 2d. It became Kit Kat in 1937. The chocolate bars are still made in York by Nestle.

4. **Aero** - launched as "the new chocolate" by Rowntree's in 1935 at a cost of 2d. They are still made in York by Nestle.

5. **Dairy Box** - launched by Rowntree's in 1936 with the advertising slogan "She'll love it if you bring her chocolates. She'll love you if they're Dairy Box".

6. **Quality Street** - launched by Macintosh's in 1936. Named after a very popular play of the same name written by J. M. Barrie (who also wrote Peter Pan). The Major and the Miss, who appeared on all Quality Street boxes and tins until 2000 were the play's principal characters.

7. **Rolo** - first sold in 1936. Made by Macintosh's.

8. **Smarties** - Rowntree's began making chocolate beans in 1882. They began calling them Smarties Chocolate Beans in 1937. Nestle makes half a million tubes per day at its York factory. The different coloured smarties all taste the same, apart from the orange ones which contain orange oil. In 2005 the famous tube was replaced with a hexitube.

9. **Black Magic** - launched in 1938 by Rowntree's as a more affordable indulgence than the very ornate and costly boxes of chocolates that were available at the time.

10. **After Eights** - created in 1962 by Rowntree's. One billion After Eights are made by Nestle in Castleford every year.

Others:

Caramac - Macintosh's 1959
Toffee Crisp - Macintosh's 1963
Munchies - Rowntree's 1957
Yorkie - Rowntree's 1976
Lion Bar - Rowntree's 1977

DRINKS

Tea, pop and beer. The whole family is catered for by famous Yorkshire brands.

Yorkshire beer has a distinctive taste. It has a bitterness and the creamy head is there to moderate this. Some of Yorkshire's greatest breweries date back to the early 1800s when industrial progress made large breweries possible. Prior to this, beer was brewed in back-of-pub brewhouses.

In the last few years the big brewers have pretty much given up on real ale to concentrate on lager, but people are getting bored of this limp, gassy drink and are returning to more traditional ales. In fact there has been an explosion in the consumption of real ale in recent years. This is great news for Yorkshire brewers such as Black Sheep and Timothy Taylor's.

According to the Campaign for Real Ale (CAMRA), West Yorkshire has more breweries producing more types of beer than any other county in the UK. In 2011 CAMRA said that the county had 43 breweries producing 276 beers. North Yorkshire was fifth on the list.

1 & 2. **Samuel Smith's and John Smith's**

Both are based in Tadcaster and share a common history. Today John Smith's is owned by Heineken, while Samuel Smith's remains independent.

Their history starts at The Old Brewery at Tadcaster, which was established in 1758 by Stephen Hartley. The brewery stayed within the Hartley family but by the 1840s was in need of investment and improvement. This was provided by John Smith who bought into the brewery in 1847. In 1852 he took it over completely and formed John Smith's Brewery.

John died childless in 1879 and his interests were inherited by his brothers William Smith and Samuel Smith. William built a new state of the art brewery next door to The Old Brewery and moved John Smith's Brewery into it. The Old Brewery passed to Samuel's son, also called Samuel, who established Samuel Smith's Brewery in 1886.

Samuel Smith's is still based in The Old Brewery. It is Yorkshire's oldest brewery. The original well at The Old Brewery is still in use, with brewing water being drawn from 85 feet underground.

Samuel Smith's ales and stouts are fermented in stone Yorkshire squares - these are like large square baths made from slabs of slate. The yeast used in the fermentation process is a strain that has been used since about 1900. In keeping with these traditions, shire horses are still used to make deliveries to local pubs.

John Smith's was taken over by Courage in 1970, which was taken over by Scottish and Newcastle, which was taken over by Heineken in 2008. Today, John Smith's Brewery at Tadcaster produces John Smith's Original, John Smith's Extra Smooth, Newcastle Brown Ale, Murphy's Irish Stout and Foster's lager and Kronenbourg 1664.

John Smith's Yorkshire Bitter is the leading brand of bitter in the country, selling over one million pints per day.

3. **Tetley's**

Founded in 1822 by Joshua Tetley in Leeds. By 1860 Tetley's was the largest brewery in the north of England. At its peak during the 1960s it employed over 1000 workers. In 1996 sales of Tetley's were overtaken by John Smith's. In 1998 Tetley's was taken over by Carlsberg. It closed Tetley's Brewery in 2011. Tetley's Smoothflow is now produced at MolsonCoors' plant in Tadcaster and Tetley cask products are brewed at Marston's in Wolverhampton.

4. **Theakston**

T & R Theakston Ltd was founded in 1827 by Robert Theakston and John Wood at The Black Bull pub in Masham. In 1987 the company was taken over by Scottish and Newcastle, but in 2004 the business returned to family ownership after being bought back from Scottish and Newcastle. Old Peculiar is Theakston's most famous beer.

5. **Black Sheep**

This brewery was born on what people in Masham call Black Sunday - The day in 1987 when T & R Theakston and Company was bought by Scottish and Newcastle Breweries. Paul Theakston decided to thumb his nose to the big breweries and go it alone. Black Sheep Brewery was named tongue-in-cheek by Paul's wife, Sue and they began brewing in 1992 in a former maltings building next door to Theakston's in Masham. The brewery produces a range of well-hopped bitters to distinguish itself from Theakston's range of fruity and yeasty beers.

6. **Timothy Taylor**

In 1858 Timothy Taylor began brewing beer in Cook Lane in Keighley. In 1863 he built a larger brewery at Knowle Spring, where the company has remained ever since. The brewery remains in the Taylor family and it produces several award winning ales such as Landlord, Taylor's Best

Bitter and Golden Best.

7. **Tetley Tea**

In 1822 Joseph and Edward Tetley started to sell salt in Yorkshire. Shortly afterwards they started to sell tea. They were so successful that they set up as tea merchants "Joseph Tetley and Co." in 1837. In 1856, to expand their business, they moved to London, which at the time was the centre of the world's tea trade. Today, the company is part of India's Tata Group. Tetley is the largest tea company in the UK.

8. **Taylors of Harrogate**

In 1886 brothers Charles and Llewellyn Taylor set up the tea and coffee importing business C. E. Taylor and Co. Llewellyn eventually became a sleeping partner and Charles hit upon the idea of opening tea and coffee tasting rooms in the booming, fashionable spa towns of Harrogate and Ilkley. The company makes Yorkshire Tea.

In 1962 Taylors was put up for sale and was bought by Bettys.

9. **Ben Shaws**

In 1871 Ben Shaw of Huddersfield left his job in the textile industry to set up his own business bottling and selling natural mineral water from the Pennine hills. He was successful and soon expanded his business introducing traditional soft drinks. If you are over 45 you may remember the pop vans that came round once a week, delivering bottles to your street. Can you remember how much money you got for returning the bottles?

10. **Fentimans**

Although based in Hexham, Northumberland, the company was founded in 1905 by Thomas Fentiman, an iron worker from Cleckheaton. He acquired a recipe for ginger beer and started selling the drink in stone jars called Grey Hens door-to-door.

The Fentimans logo is based on Fearless, Thomas Fentiman's prize alsation, double winner of Crufts' obedience test.

The company closed down in the mid 1960s as supermarkets started selling soft drinks. In 1988 Eldon Robson, great grandson of Thomas Fentiman, re-established the company with a mission to produce drinks using the original recipes.

FAMOUS YORKSHIRE FOODS

Yorkshire has a very rich food culture. Of course there's Yorkshire pudding, but Tykes have always enjoyed their desserts and sweets. As a result a large number of the most traditional Yorkshire recipes are for desserts.

1. **Yorkshire pudding**
   The Yorkshire pudding originated in Yorkshire and is made from batter. It is a staple of the British Sunday lunch. The first recipe for a "dripping pudding" appeared in 1737.

2. **Ginger beer**
   Yorkshire was the birthplace of ginger beer, although this was originally an alcoholic drink. It has existed since the mid 1700s.

3. **Yorkshire Parkin**
   Parkin is the Yorkshire form of gingerbread, made with oatmeal and treacle or molasses. It's traditionally eaten on Bonfire Night. The first written mention of parkin seems to be in the journal of Dorothy Wordsworth (sister of the poet

William) in 1800, although the cake must have been in existence for a long time before that.

4. **Yorkshire Forced Rhubarb**
   Traditionally grown by candlelight in the "Rhubarb Triangle" - an area between Wakefield, Leeds and Bradford. In 2010 it was awarded Protected Designation of Origin status by the European Commission. Other protected names include Stilton Cheese, Parma Ham and Champagne.

   The cultivation method for forced rhubarb was developed in the early 1800s. The rhubarb plant spends two years growing outside where its leaves produce sugars which are stored in the roots. The plants are then placed inside huts in complete darkness. The huts are heated and this forces the rhubarb to mobilize its stored sugar and grow long sweet stalks. This forced rhubarb is more tender than rhubarb grown outside in summer.

   Rhubarb is enjoying a resurgence in popularity. It has a high calcium content and is popular with dieters because it is a metabolism booster.

5. **Yorkshire curd tart**
   This has been around since the 1750s. They were originally made from the fresh curds left over from cheese making. Curd tarts are made in other parts of the country, but the Yorkshire version was unique because it included rosewater.

6. **Fat rascals**
   Also called the Yorkshire tea biscuit or turf cake. They are a cross between a cake and a scone. They originated in northern Yorkshire, possibly as far back as Elizabethan times.

7. **Yorkshire brack**
   This is a fruit cake made with tea and sometimes whisky. No added fat is used.

8. **Growlers**

   This is the Yorkshire name for pork pies. A large family sized pork pie is known as a stand pie. Ripponden holds an annual charity pork pie competition for small, independent butchers and bakers. It's organised by the pork pie appreciation society.

9. **Wensleydale cheese**

   Wensleydale Cheese has been made in Wensleydale since 1150 when Cistercian monks settled in the dale and established a monastery at Fors, four miles from Hawes. Their methods were passed on to local farmers' wives. Today, the cheese is made at the Wensleydale Creamery in Hawes to a time-honoured recipe that uses milk from local farms.

10. **Yorkshire ham**

    It's also called York ham if it's produced within the citadel of York. It traditionally comes from the Large White pig. The ham is dry cured which gives the meat a distinctive salty flavour and dry texture.

    Yorkshire ham doesn't have protected regional status, so any ham made anywhere can be called Yorkshire ham so long as it's cured to the Yorkshire ham method.

Foods made in Yorkshire today

1. **Coca-Cola**
   The iconic Coca-Cola can is manufactured in Outwood, Wakefield in the largest soft drinks factory in Europe. The factory makes 100 million cans every year and employs over 500 people.

2. **Nestle**
   The world's largest food company, based in the Swiss town of Vevey. Nestle has factories in York, Castleford and Halifax. York makes kit kats, aeros, yorkies, milky bars and polos. Castleford makes toffee crisp. Halifax makes walnut whips, quality street and rolo biscuits.

3. **Kraft Foods**
   Kraft bought Cadbury in 2011. In 1989 Cadbury had taken over Bassett's. Cadbury also took over Maynard's. Today, Kraft produces Liquorice Allsorts, Jelly Babies and Maynard's Wine Gums in Sheffield.

4. **KP Nuts**
   Produced in Eastwood which is north of Rotherham.

5. **Fox's Biscuits**
   Still made in Batley. The factory produces a huge range of biscuits that includes Rocky, Echo, Sports Biscuits, Party Rings.

6. **Aunt Bessie's frozen Yorkshire puddings**
   Made in Hull. Aunt Bessie's is the world's largest producer of frozen yorkshire puddings. The Hull factory produces over 20 million puddings each week.

7. **Haribo**
   The German company has a factory in Pontefract. Not

surprisingly it produces Pontefract Cakes as well as other sweets. The factory employs over 500 people.

8. **R&R Ice Cream**
   The company produces over 600 million ice lollies every year at its factory in Leeming Bar. The company holds the licence to make a range of Nestle ices - these include FAB, Rolo, Fruit Pastilles, Smarties and Toffee Crisp. It also makes Thorntons Ice Cream and Ribena ice lollies. 450 people work at the factory.

9. **Marlow Foods,** Stokesley
   Makers of Quorn. The mycoprotein products are named after the Leicestershire village of Quorn. Quorn is made from the soil mould Fusarium venenatum.

10. **Seabrook** crisps are made in Bradford

Also:

McCain makes its frozen chips in Scarborough.
Seven Seas makes cod liver oil capsules and multivitamins at Marfleet in Hull
Dalepak at Leeming Bar produces a range of grills, ribsteaks and burgers.

MISCELLANEOUS

Largest railway stations

Figures are for annual rail passenger usage for 2010

1. **Leeds** 17 platforms. Third busiest station outside of London after Birmingham New Street and Glasgow Central. 22 million.
2. **Sheffield** 9 platforms. 7.5 million.
3. **York** 11 platforms. 6.9 million.
4. **Huddersfield** 6 platforms. 3.8 million.
5. **Doncaster** 8 platforms 3.7 million
6. **Wakefield Westgate** 2 platforms 2.3 million
7. **Bradford Interchange** 4 platforms 2.3 million
8. **Hull Paragon Interchange** 7 platforms. 2.1 million.
9. **Bradford Forster Square** 3 platforms 2.1 million
10. **Meadowhall Interchange** 4 platforms 1.8 million

Famous (non-food) companies founded in Yorkshire

1. **Marks and Spencer**
   Founded in 1884 by Michael Marks and Thomas Spencer in Leeds.

2. **Waddingtons**
   Founded by John Waddington of Leeds in the 19th Century. The company began as a printers. In 1922 it began making playing cards. In the 1930s Waddingtons started producing Monopoly and in 1949 Cluedo was brought out. In 1994 Waddingtons was bought by American company Hasbro.

3. **Asda**
   Asda was founded in 1965 in Leeds when two companies merged. These were the Asquith chain of three supermarkets and Associated Dairies and Farm Stores Ltd. Asda is an abbreviation of Asquith and Dairies. In 1999 Asda became a subsidiary of American retail giant Walmart, which is the world's largest retailer.

4. **Morrisons**
   Founded in 1899 by William Morrison. The company began as an egg and butter stall in Rawson Market in Bradford. His son, Ken Morrison took over the company in 1952. In 1958 Ken opened a small shop in the city centre. The first Morrisons supermarket opened in 1961 in the Girlington district of Bradford.

5. **Comet**
   Began by George Hollingberry in Hull in 1933 as Comet Battery Stores Ltd.

6. **Next**
   The company was founded by Joseph Hepworth in Leeds in 1864 as Joseph Hepworth and Son, Gentleman's Tailors. In 1981 Hepworth's bought the chain of Kendall's rainswear shops and rebranded them as Next, selling womenswear. In 1986 the company J Hepworth and Son changed its name to Next plc.

7. **Persimmon plc**
   Founded in 1972 in York by Duncan Davidson. The company is named after a horse that in 1896 won the Derby and St. Leger. Persimmon is one of the country's largest house builders.

8. **Silver Cross**
   In 1877 William Wilson invented the modern pram. It had a reversible hood and spring suspension. Wilson's

perambulator was truly revolutionary and at first he made them at Silver Cross Street, Hunslet, Leeds. In 1936 the company took over an old silk factory in Guiseley. The company collapsed in 2002 following the discovery of £3million of financial irregularities in its accounts. The factory closed and was demolished to make way for a housing estate. Silver Cross was bought by David Halsall International and production moved to Bingley and its headquarters to Broughton Hall near Skipton.

9. **GHD**

This name might not mean much to male readers, but to female ones, especially those with long hair, GHD is a very important company. GHD stands for good hair day. GHD makes and sells hair straighteners of the very highest quality. The company was founded in Ilkley in 2001 by Martin Penny, Gary Douglas and Robert Powls. The three collaborated to purchase the rights to manufacture a particular type of ceramic hair straightening iron from a South Korean inventor.

10. **Wharfedale**

The company is famous the world over for producing high quality speakers and hi-fi equipment. In 1932 Gilbert Briggs built his first loudspeaker in the cellar of his home in Ilkley, which is in Wharfedale. In 1933 Briggs set up a small factory near Bradford to produce speakers.

Facts about Yorkshire

1. **The emblem of Yorkshire** is the white rose of the historical royal House of York and the most commonly used flag representative of Yorkshire is the white rose on a dark blue background.

2. **Yorkshire Day** is held on August 1st and is a celebration of Yorkshire culture.

3. **The 1991 census** put the population of Yorkshire and Humberside at 5.3 million.

4. **The county is so named** because it is the shire (administrative area or county) of the city of York. It is York's shire. "York" comes from the Viking name for the city, Jorvik.

5. **The title Duke of York**, a title of nobility in British peerage, was created in 1385, but was merged with the Crown when the 4th Duke became King Edward IV in 1461. Since then, the title of Duke of York has usually been given to the second son of the King or Queen.

6. **The name, Yorkshire**, first appeared in writing in the Anglo-Saxon Chronicle in 1065.

7. **The term "Riding"** comes from the Viking word threthingr, which means a third. There has never been a south riding. South Yorkshire was created in 1974 and was taken from the West Riding.

8. **Many of our words** and place names are Viking in origin:

Word	Meaning	Old Norse
bairn	child	barn
laik	play	leike
beck	stream	bekkr
arse	bottom	ars
dale	valley	dalur
fell	hill	fjall
flit	move house	flytja
gawp	to stare	gapa
muck	dirt	myki

Places names:

-by - means village
-thorpe - old Norse word for small village or farmstead
-thwaite - means clearing in a forest or meadow

9. **According to the Ordnance Survey**, the geographical centre of Yorkshire is the village of Hessay near York.

10. **At 6,000 square miles**, Yorkshire is Britain's largest county.

Great Yorkshire sayings

1. **Tha' can allus tell a Yorkshireman, but tha' can't tell 'im much**

2. **Ee, by gum**

3. **Wheere ther's muck, ther's brass**

4. **'Ey up**

5. **It's neither nowt nor summat**

6. **Sit thissen dahn an' tell me abaht it**

7. **See all, 'ear all, say nowt. Eat all, sup all, pay nowt. An' if th'ivver does owt for nowt, allus do it for thissen**

8. **Well, Ah'll go to t'foot of ahr stairs**

9. **Put t'wood in t'oil**

10. **An' Ah'll tell thi that fer nowt**

YORKSHIRE FIRSTS

1. **Helen Sharman**
   She was born in Sheffield in 1963. She became the first Briton in space when she visited the Mir space station aboard Soyuz TM-12 in 1991.

2. **Amy Johnson**
   Born in Hull in 1903, she was the first woman to fly solo from Britain to Australia in 1930.

3. **Alan Hinkes**
   Born in Northallerton in 1954. Hinkes was the first British mountaineer to reach the summit of all 14 mountains with elevations greater than 8000 metres.

4. **Brian Robinson**
   Born in Huddersfield in 1930 he was the first Briton to finish the Tour de France and the first Briton to win a Tour stage.

5. **Barbara Jane Harrison**
   Born in Bradford in 1945. Died 1968. The first and only woman to be awarded the George Cross medal for gallantry in peacetime. She was awarded the medal posthumously in 1969. She was a stewardess on a flight from London Heathrow to Sydney. Shortly after take-off one of the plane's engines caught fire and fell off. The plane managed to land and the fire spread to the fuselage. Harrison helped passengers to escape and refused to leave the burning aircraft until everyone was saved. Her body was found near that of a disabled pensioner seated in one of the last rows.

   Her George Cross is now located at British Airways' Speedbird Centre which is dedicated to the history of the crew and story of British Airways.

6. **Fred Trueman**
   Born in Stainton in 1931. He was the first bowler to take 300 test wickets.

7. **Footballing firsts:**
(i) World's first inter-club football match was held on 26th December 1860. It was between two Sheffield clubs, Sheffield FC (which is the oldest football club in the world, founded in 1857) and Hallam FC (the second oldest football club in the world, founded in 1860). The match was played at Hallam FC's Sandygate ground which is the oldest football ground in the world.
(i) In 1866 Sheffield FC and London City play the first inter-city match at Battersea Park.
(iii) Herbert Chapman was first manager to win the division 1 title with two different clubs - Huddersfield in 1924 and 1925 and Arsenal in 1931 and 1933 with Arsenal.
(iv) Brian Clough was the first and only British manager to win successive European Cups. This he did with Nottingham Forest in 1979 and 1980.

8. **Bradford** was designated as the world's first UNESCO City of Film in 2009. The title was awarded because of the city's rich film heritage, its inspirational movie locations and its many celebrations of the moving image through the National Media Museum and the city's annual film festivals.

9. **James Cook**
(i) In 1770 he was the first European to visit the east coast of Australia. Cook claimed it for Britain and called it New South Wales. He was also the first to visit the Hawaiian islands, where unfortunately he was killed in a fight with locals.
(ii) First to circumnavigate New Zealand.
(iii) First to cross the Antarctic circle and circumnavigate Antarctica in 1773, though he never spotted land.

(iv) Yorkshire's greatest son was also the first to circumnavigate the globe in both directions and the first to prevent scurvy on long voyages.

10. **In 1853 Sir George Cayley** built the first practical heavier-than-air flying machine. It was a glider that his coach driver flew 900 feet across a small valley. This was the first recorded flight by a person in an aircraft and Cayley has been described as the "true inventor of the aeroplane".

And:

Ben Shaws of Huddersfield was the first company in Europe to can soft drinks in 1959.

YORKSHIRE RECORDS

1. **Charlotte Marion Hughes**, née Milburn (1 August 1877–17 March 1993) is the longest-lived person ever documented in the United Kingdom at 115 years 228 days. She was born and grew up in Middlesbrough where her father ran a music shop. Charlotte was the third undisputed person in history to reach age 115.

2. **The Olde Sweet Shop** in Pateley Bridge, established 1827, is England's oldest sweet shop. It's found at the top of the High Street. It's hardly changed over the last 200 years and it has over 200 jars of sweets on display.

(Yorkshire also has the smallest shop in Britain - The Little Shop is part of The George and Dragon pub in Hudswell near Richmond. The pub's beer garden has great views of Swaledale.)

3. **Largest serving of fish and chips**
   On 2nd July 2011 staff at the Wensleydale Heifer pub in West Witton, North Yorkshire, set a world record for the largest serving of fish and chips. The halibut, which in accordance with Guinness Book rules, was fried as a single fish, weighed 44 lbs and the chips added another 52 lbs. The AA award-winning pub is a 17th Century inn, named as one of the UK top 20 restaurants with rooms in 2011 by The Sunday Times.

4. **Yorkshire County Cricket Club** have been county champions the most times - 30 plus one shared. Lancashire? Only eight plus one shared.

5. **Hedley Verity**. In 1932, in a game against Nottinghamshire, he took ten wickets for ten runs. This is still the record in first class cricket for the fewest runs conceded while taking all ten wickets.

6. **Wilfred Rhodes** from Kirkheaton holds a number of cricketing records. He played 58 Test matches for England between 1899 and 1930. Rhodes took 127 wickets and scored 2,325 runs, becoming the first Englishman to complete the double of 1,000 runs and 100 wickets in Test matches. He holds the world records both for the most appearances made in first-class cricket (1,110 matches) and for the most wickets taken (4,204). He completed the double of 1,000 runs and 100 wickets in an English cricket season a record 16 times. Rhodes played for Yorkshire and England into his fifties, and in his final Test in 1930 was, at 52 years and 165 days, the oldest player who has appeared in a Test match.

7. **The Kiplingcotes Derby** is the oldest annual horse race in England. It began in 1519 and takes place on the third Thursday in March. Kiplingcotes is a small hamlet close to

Market Weighton.

The rules of the race state that if the race is not run one year then it must never be run again. During the harsh winter of 1947 no one was daring enough to take part and so one local farmer lead a lone horse around the course, ensuring that the historic race would survive. During the 2001 foot and mouth crisis the race was once again reduced to one horse and rider.

The St. Leger, run at Doncaster in September, is the oldest of the British Classics. It was first run in 1776.

8. **Standedge Tunnel** - it's the longest, highest and deepest canal tunnel in the UK. It's 3.25 miles long and it runs through the Pennine hills between Marsden and Diggle. Before 1974 Diggle was part of the West Riding, but now it's part of Greater Manchester.

   (Dent is the highest railway station in England. In 1974 Dent was taken from the West Riding and given to Cumbria)

9. **Last of the Summer Wine** is the longest running sitcom in the world. It ran from 1973 to 2010. There were 31 series and 295 episodes. Every episode was written by Roy Clarke. It was filmed in and around Holmfirth.

10. In 2010 archaeologists discovered **Britain's oldest house** at a site near Scarborough. The 3.5m diameter house has been dated as being made in 8,500 BC.

Also:

Huddersfield Town Football Club holds the record for the longest unbeaten run in the English Football League. The run of 43 matches lasted for 336 days. There were 25 wins and 18 draws. The run came to an end on the 28th of November, 2011 with a 2-0 defeat away to Charlton

Athletic. The run eclipsed Nottingham Forest's run of 42 games in 1977-78. Arsenal's run of 49 games unbeaten is a Premiership record. Huddersfield's record is for the Football League.

Aakash in Cleckheaton is the largest Indian restaurant in the world.

Wentworth Woodhouse has the longest country house facade in Europe. Its east front is 606 feet (185m) long. The house is privately owned but you can visit the surrounding parkland as it is owned and managed by Rotherham Council. The 365 room house was the former seat of the Second Marquess of Rockingham, who was twice prime minister.

York Minster is the largest gothic cathedral in northern Europe.

The Great East Window at York Minster is the world's largest single expanse of medieval stained glass.

The Battle of Towton was fought during the Wars of the Roses on March 29th 1461. It was the largest and bloodiest battle ever fought on British soil. More than 80,000 soldiers of the houses of York and Lancaster fought for several hours during a snow storm on what was Palm Sunday. Nearly 30,000 died. The battle was won by the Yorkists. Towton is near Tadcaster.

THINGS THAT YORKSHIRE HAS GIVEN THE WORLD

My first thoughts were Yorkshire puddings and John Smith's and Tetley's beers. When I sobered up I realised that Yorkshire has been responsible for some even greater achievements.

1. **Football**
   FIFA has recognised Sheffield as being the birthplace of club football.

2. **Rugby League**
   In 1895, a schism in rugby football resulted in the formation of the Northern Rugby Football Union. Twenty-two clubs met at the George Hotel, Huddersfield and formed the NRFU.

3. **Flight**
   Sir George Cayley (born Scarborough 1773) designed the first successful glider to carry a human being aloft and he discovered and identified the four aerodynamic forces of flight: weight, lift, drag, and thrust. Modern aeroplane design is based on those discoveries.

4. **Modern computers**
   Tom Kilburn (born Dewsbury 1921), in 1948, produced the first computer software and this allowed the development of modern computers.

5. **Nuclear power**
   Sir John Cockcroft, along with Ernest Walton, was the first to split the atomic nucleus in 1932. Cockcroft was born in Todmorden in 1897 and Walton was an Irishman. Working at the Cavendish Laboratory at Cambridge University, they focused a beam of protons onto lithium atoms to break apart their nuclei. In order to do this they had to create the

world's first nuclear particle accelerator. This machine produced the beam of protons. A lithium nucleus is made up from three protons and four neutrons. When a high speed proton hit the lithium nucleus it caused it to split and form two new helium nuclei each made up from two protons and two neutrons. It was the first nuclear transmutation of one element (lithium) into another (helium) under full human control. Calculations that followed their experiment confirmed Einstein's law $E=mc^2$.

Cockcroft and Walton received the Nobel Prize for Physics in 1951 for their experiment. Their work led to the development of nuclear power with Cockcroft playing a large part in this as the first director of the Atomic Energy Research Establishment at Harwell, Oxfordshire.

6. **Fizzy drinks**
Carbonation (the fizz is carbon dioxide bubbles) was invented by Joseph Priestley (born Birstall 1733).

7. **Pain free operations**
John Snow (born York 1813) pioneered the use of ether and chloroform as anaesthetics.

8. **Safe and accurate navigation at sea**
This was made possible by the invention of the marine chronometer by John Harrison (born Foulby near Wakefield 1693). To navigate at sea both latitude and longitude need to be calculated. Time of day must be known to calculate longitude but producing a timepiece that would work at sea was a great challenge. So much so that the British government passed the Longitude Act of 1714 that offered a prize of £20,000 (worth about £3 million today) for the solution. The first true maritime chronometer was the life work of one man, John Harrison, spanning 31 years of persistent experimentation and test. His invention enabled the age of discovery and colonialism to accelerate.

9. **Stainless steel**
   Invented in 1912 by Harry Brearley (born Sheffield 1871) of the Brown-Firth research laboratory in Sheffield while seeking a corrosion-resistant alloy for gun barrels.

10. **Safer roads**
   Percy Shaw (born Halifax 1890) invented cat's eyes in 1934.

Plus:

Thanksgiving Day in the USA. William Bradford (born in Austerfield in 1590) was a leader of settlers at Plymouth Colony in Massachusetts. They were the pilgrims who had sailed to America in 1620 aboard the Mayflower. Bradford served as governor there for 30 years and was the first to designate what is now known as Thanksgiving Day.

My favourite places in Yorkshire

My three favourite pastimes feature quite a lot in this list. They are eating, drinking and dog walking.

1. **Magpie Cafe, Whitby**
   Fish and chips is my favourite food and this is my favourite place to eat them. My partner Kate and I usually go mid-afternoon to avoid the queues.

2. **Brimham Rocks**
   The dogs love this place and the views of Nidderdale are fantastic.

3. **Middleham Moor**
   There's a track around the gallops that gives fine views of Coverdale on one side and Wensleydale on the other side.

4. **Bolton Abbey**
   I usually park near Bolton Bridge and walk along the river to the abbey and then the Cavendish Pavilion riverside cafe. If I want a longer walk I carry on to the Strid or even Barden Bridge. I can't think of many nicer riverside walks.

5. **Canon Hall Farm**
   Brilliant place for kids and adults alike. Go in spring when the kid goats and lambs are causing trouble.

6. **York Minster**
   One of the great cathedrals of the world. Just a marvel of Middle Ages construction. The views from the top of the central tower are worth the climb.

7. **The Blacksmiths Arms, Kirkheaton, near Mirfield**
   Go there just for the far reaching views over Huddersfield and the Pennine hills beyond.

8. **Simonstone Hall near Hawes**
   Beautiful hotel and a great place to go just for a drive and a meal if you live anywhere near.

9. **Farah's shop in Harrogate**
   I've never been to a better sweet shop.

10. **Ingleborough summit**
    An easy mountain to climb and the views are spectacular.